KARL MARX

PRE-CAPITALIST ECONOMIC FORMATIONS

KARL MARX
PRE-CAPITALIST ECONOMIC FORMATIONS

translated by
JACK COHEN

edited and with an Introduction by
E. J. HOBSBAWM

INTERNATIONAL PUBLISHERS
NEW YORK

© (1964) *E. J. Hobsbawn (Introduction), J. Cohen (Translation)*
First United States Edition, International Publishers, 1965
All Rights Reserved

This printing 2018

Library of Congress Catalog Card Number: 65-16393

(paperback) ISBN-13: 978-0-7178-0165-7

Printed in the United States

Note on Texts, References and Translation

THE main text of Marx presented here is the notes *Formen die der Kapitalistischen Produktion vorhergehen (über den Prozess der der Bildung des Kapitalverhaltnisses oder der Ursprünglichen Akkumulation vorhergeht)*, supplemented by some extracts from *The German Ideology* of Marx and Engels, and from their Correspondence.

In the translation of the *Formen*, Marx's paragraphs, which are sometimes excessively long, have been broken up. Marx's own divisions are indicated by an asterisk at the beginning of the paragraph. Possible ambiguities in the translation are noted in footnotes. Marx's own footnotes are marked as such. Passages in foreign languages other than German have also been translated, unless they are merely technical terms such as *ager publicus*. Passages inserted in English in Marx's original text have been left unchanged. Italicised passages and words indicate emphasis by Marx.

The references made in the Introduction to other writings of Marx and Engels are mainly to the thirty-volume—but at the time of writing uncomplete—*Karl Marx, Friedrich Engels, Werke* (Dietz Verlag, Berlin, 1956—). This is cited as *Werke*. Since the relevant volumes are not yet available at the time of writing, references to *Capital* III are to the Dietz Verlag edition of 1956 and letters are merely identified by date, writer and recipient. *Capital* I is quoted from the Dona Torr edition (Allen and Unwin, 1938) of the English translation edited by Engels.

E. J. H.

Contents

Introduction

I

THE present work is a section of a bulky manuscript composed by Marx in 1857-8 in preparation for his *Critique of Political Economy* and *Capital*. This was published under the title *Grundrisse der Kritik der Politischen Ökonomie* in Moscow, 1939-41, though some small extracts had appeared in the *Neue Zeit* in 1903. The time and place of publication caused the work to be virtually unknown until 1952 when the present section of it was published as a pamphlet in Berlin, and 1953, when the entire *Grundrisse* were republished in the same city. This 1953 German edition remains the only accessible one. I know of no translations into West European languages other than Italian (1956). The *Grundrisse* thus belong to that large group of Marx and Engels manuscripts which were never published during their authors' lifetime, and have become available for adequate study only since 1930. Most of them, such as the *Economic-Philosophical Manuscripts of 1844*, which have figured a great deal in recent discussions, belong to the youth of both Marx and Marxism. The *Grundrisse*, however, belong to his full maturity. They are the outcome of a decade of intensive study in England, and clearly represent the stage of his thought which immediately precedes the drafting of *Capital* during the early 1860s, for which, as already observed, they provide preliminary work. The *Grundrisse* are therefore the last major writings of the mature Marx to have reached the public.

Under the circumstances, their neglect is very surprising. This is especially true of the sections, headed

Formen die der Kapitalistischen Produktion vorhergehen, in which Marx attempts to grapple with the problem of pre-capitalist historic evolution, and which are translated here. For these are not unimportant or casual notes. The present work does not merely represent—as Marx himself proudly wrote to Lassalle (November 12, 1858)—"the result of fifteen years' research, that is to say of the best years of my life". It not only shows Marx at his most brilliant and profound. It is also in many ways his most systematic attempt to grapple with the problem of historic evolution and the indispensable pendant to the superb Preface to the *Critique of Political Economy,* which was written shortly after and presents historical materialism in its most pregnant form. It can be said without hesitation that any Marxist historical discussion which does not take into account the present work—that is to say virtually all such discussion before 1941, and (unfortunately) much of it since—must be reconsidered in its light.

There are, however, obvious reasons for this neglect. The *Grundrisse* were, as Marx wrote to Lassalle, "monographs, written at widely varying periods, for my own clarification and not for publication". Not only do they require from the reader an easy familiarity with Marx's idiom of thought—i.e. with his entire intellectual evolution and especially with Hegelianism—but they are also written in a sort of private intellectual shorthand which is sometimes impenetrable, in the form of rough notes interspersed with asides which, however clear they may have been to Marx, are often ambiguous to us. Anyone who has tried to translate the manuscript or even to study and interpret it, will know that it is sometimes quite impossible to put the meaning of some sibylline passage beyond all reasonable doubt.

Even if Marx had taken the trouble to make his meaning clear, it would still be far from easy, because his analysis is conducted at a very high level of generality, that is to say in highly abstract terms. In the first place Marx is here concerned—as in the Preface to the *Critique*—to establish the general mechanism of *all* social change: the formation of social relations of production which correspond to a definite stage of development of the material forces of production; the periodic development of conflicts between the forces and relations of production; the 'epochs of social revolution' in which the relations once again adjust themselves to the level of the forces. This general analysis does not imply any statement about specific historical periods, forces and relations of productions whatever. Thus the word 'class' is not even mentioned in the Preface, for classes are merely special cases of social relations of production at particular—though admittedly very long—periods of history. And the only actual statement about historic formations and periods, is the brief, unsupported and unexplained list of the "epochs in the progress of the economic formation of society"—namely, the "Asiatic, ancient, feudal and modern bourgeois", of which the final one is the last "antagonistic" form of the social process of production.

The *Formen* are both more general and more specific than the Preface, though they too—it is important to note this at the outset—are not "history" in the strict sense. In one aspect, the draft attempts to discover in the analysis of social evolution the characteristics of *any* dialectical, or indeed of any satisfying, theory on any subject whatever. It seeks to possess, and indeed it does possess, those qualities of intellectual economy, generality and unbroken internal logic, which scientists incline to call "beauty" or "elegance", and it pursues them, by the use of Hegel's dialectical method, though on a materialist and not an idealist basis.

This immediately brings us to the second aspect.

The *Formen* seek to formulate the *content* of history in its most general form. This content is *progress*. Neither those who deny the existence of historical progress nor those who (often basing themselves on the writings of the immature Marx) see Marx's thought merely as an ethical demand for the liberation of man, will find any support here. For Marx progress is something objectively definable, and at the same time pointing to what is desirable. The strength of the Marxist belief in the triumph of the free development of all men, depends not on the strength of Marx's hope for it, but on the assumed correctness of the analysis that this is indeed where historical development eventually leads mankind.

The objective basis of Marx's humanism, but of course also, and simultaneously, of his theory of social and economic evolution, is his analysis of man as a social animal. Man—or rather men—perform *labour*, i.e. they create and reproduce their existence in daily practice, breathing, seeking food, shelter, love, etc. They do this by operating *in* nature, taking from nature (and eventually consciously changing nature) for this purpose. This interaction between man and nature is, and produces, social evolution. Taking from nature, or determining the use of some bit of nature (including one's own body), can be, and indeed is in common parlance, seen as appropriation, which is therefore originally merely an aspect of labour. It is expressed in the concept of *property* (which is not by any means the same thing as the historically special case of *private* property). In the beginning, says Marx, "the relationship of the worker to the objective conditions of his labour is one of ownership; this is the natural unity of labour with its material (*sachliche*) prerequisites" (p. 67). Being a social animal man develops both co-operation and a *social division of labour* (i.e. specialisation of functions), which is not only made possible by, but increases the further possibilities of, producing a *surplus* over and above what is needed to maintain the individual and the community of which he is a part. The existence of both the surplus and the social division of labour makes possible *exchange*. But initially both production and exchange have as their object merely *use*—i.e. the maintenance of the producer and his community. These are the main analytical bricks out of which the theory is built, and all are in fact expansions or corollaries of, the original concept of man as a social animal of a special kind.[1]

Progress of course is observable in the growing emancipation of man from nature and his growing control over nature. This emancipation—i.e. from the situation as given when primitive men go about their living, and from the original and spontaneous (or as Marx says *naturwüchsig*—'as grown up in nature') relations which emerge from the process of the evolution of animals into human groups—affects not only the forces but also the relations of production. And it is with the latter aspect that the *Formen* deals. On the one hand, the relations men enter into as a result of the specialisation of labour—and notably *exchange*—are progressively clarified and sophisticated, until the invention of *money* and with it of *commodity production* and exchange, provides a basis for procedures unimaginable before, including capital accumulation. This process, while mentioned at the outset of the present essay (p. 67), is not its major subject. On the other, the double relation of labour-property is progressively broken up, as man moves further from the *naturwüchsig* or spontaneously evolved primitive relation with nature. It takes the form of a progressive

[1] For Engels' explanation of the evolution of man from apes, and hence of the difference between man and the other primates, cf. his 1876 draft on "The part of labour in the transformation of the ape into man" in the *Dialectics of Nature*, Werke, XX, 444-55.

"separation of free labour from the objective conditions of its realisation—from the means of labour
(*Arbeitsmittel*) and the material of labour. . . . Hence,
above all, the separation of the labourer from the earth
as his natural laboratory" (p. 67). Its final clarification
is achieved under capitalism, when the worker is
reduced to nothing but labour-power, and conversely,
we may add, property to a control of the means of
production entirely divorced from labour, while in the
process of production there is a total separation between use (which has no direct relevance) and exchange
and accumulation (which is the direct object of production). This is the process which, in its possible
variations of type, Marx attempts to analyse here.
Though particular social-economic formations, expressing particular phases of this evolution, are very
relevant, it is the entire process, spanning the centuries
and continents, which he has in mind. Hence his
framework is chronological only in the broadest sense,
and problems of, let us say, the transition from one
phase to another, are not his primary concern, except
in so far as they throw light on the long-term transformation.

But at the same time this process of the emancipation
of man from his original natural conditions of production is one of human *individualisation*. "Man is only
individualised (*vereinzelt sich*) through the process of
history. He appears originally as a generic being, a
tribal being, a herd animal. . . . Exchange itself is a
major agent of this individualisation. It makes the
herd animal superfluous and dissolves it" (p. 96).
This automatically implies a transformation in the
relations of the individual to what was originally
the community in which he functioned. The former
community has been transmuted, in the extreme case
of capitalism, into the dehumanised social mechanism
which, while it actually makes individualisation possible,

is outside and hostile to the individual. And yet this process is one of immense possibilities for humanity. As Marx observes in a passage full of hope and splendour (p. 84-5):

"The ancient conception, in which man always appears (in however narrowly national, religious or political a definition) as the aim of production, seems very much more exalted than the modern world, in which production is the aim of man and wealth the aim of production. In fact, however, when the narrow bourgeois form has been peeled away, what is wealth, if not the universality of needs, capacities, enjoyments, productive powers, etc., of individuals, produced in universal exchange? What, if not the full development of human control over the forces of nature—those of his own nature as well as those of so-called 'nature'? What, if not the absolute elaboration of his creative dispositions, without any preconditions other than antecedent historical evolution which makes the totality of this evolution— i.e. the evolution of all human powers as such, unmeasured by any *previously established* yardstick— an end in itself? What is this, if not a situation where man does not reproduce himself in any determined form, but produces his totality? Where he does not seek to remain something formed by the past, but is in the absolute movement of becoming? In bourgeois political economy—and in the epoch of production to which it corresponds—this complete elaboration of what lies within man appears as the total alienation, and the destruction of all fixed, one-sided purposes as the sacrifice of the end in itself to a wholly external compulsion."

Even in this most dehumanised and apparently contradictory form, the humanist ideal of free individual development is nearer than it ever was in all previous phases of history. It only awaits the passage from what Marx calls, in a lapidary phrase, the prehistoric stage of human society—the age of class societies of which capitalism is the last—to the age when man is in control of his fate, the age of communism.

Marx's vision is thus a marvellously unifying force. His model of social and economic development is one which (unlike Hegel's) can be applied to history to produce fruitful and original results rather than tautology; but at the same time it can be presented as the unfolding of the logical possibilities latent in a few elementary and almost axiomatic statements about the nature of man—a dialectical working out of the contradictions of labour/property, and the division of labour.[1] It is a model of facts, but, seen from a slightly different angle, the *same* model provides us with value-judgments. It is this multi-dimensionality of Marx's theory which causes all but the dim-witted or prejudiced to respect and admire Marx as a thinker, even when they do not agree with him. At the same time, especially when Marx himself makes no concessions to the requirements of an outside reader, it undoubtedly adds to the difficulty of this text.

One example of this complexity must be particularly mentioned: it is Marx's refusal to separate the different academic disciplines. It is possible to do so in his stead. Thus the late J. Schumpeter, one of the more intelligent critics of Marx, attempted to distinguish Marx the sociologist from Marx the economist, and one could easily separate out Marx the historian. But such mechanical divisions are misleading, and entirely contrary to Marx's method. It was the bourgeois

[1] Marx—unlike Hegel—is not taken in by the possibility—and indeed, at certain stages of thought, the necessity—of an abstract and *a priori* presentation of his theory. Cf. the section—brilliant, profound and exciting as almost everything Marx wrote in this crucial period of his thought—on The Method of political economy, in the (unpublished) Introduction to the *Critique of Political Economy* (*Werke*, XIII, 631-9), where he discusses the value of this procedure.

academic economists who attempted to draw a sharp
line between static and dynamic analysis, hoping to
transform the one into the other by injecting some
'dynamising' element into the static system, just as it
is the academic economists who still work out a neat
model of 'economic growth', preferably expressible in
equations, and relegate all that does not fit into the
province of the 'sociologists'. The academic sociologists make similar distinctions on a rather lower
level of scientific interest, the historians on an even
humbler one. But this is not Marx's way. The social
relations of production (i.e. social organisation in its
broadest sense) and the material forces of production,
to whose level they correspond, cannot be divorced.
"The economic structure of society is formed by the
totality of these relations of production" (Preface,
Werke, XIII, 8). Economic development cannot be
simplified down into 'economic growth', still less into
the variation of isolated factors such as productivity or
the rate of capital accumulation, in the way of the
modern vulgar economist who used to argue that
growth is produced when more than, say, 5 per cent
of the national income is invested.[1] It cannot be discussed except in terms of particular historic epochs and
particular social structures. The discussion of various
pre-capitalist modes of production in this essay is a
brilliant example of this, and incidentally illustrates
how entirely wrong it is to think of historical materialism as an *economic* (or for that matter a *sociological*)
interpretation of history.[2]

[1] Marx was perfectly aware of the possibility of such simplifications and, though
he did not rate them as too important, their use. Hence his suggestion that a study of
the historic growth of productivity might be a way of giving some scientific significance to Adam Smith's aperçus on stagnant and progressive economies. Introduction
to the *Critique of Political Economy*, I, 1 *Werke*, 618.
[2] This is recognised by the abler critics of Marxism. Thus G. Lichtheim correctly
points out that the sociological theories of Max Weber—on religion and capitalism or
oriental society—are not alternatives to Marx. They are either anticipated by him, or
can readily be fitted into his framework. *Marxism* (1961) 385; 'Marx and the Asiatic
Mode of Production" (*St. Antony's Papers*, 14, 1963), 106.

Yet even if we are firmly aware that Marx must not be divided up into segments according to the academic specialisations of our time, it may still be difficult to grasp the unity of his thought, partly because the mere effort at systematic and lucid exposition tends to lead us to discuss its different aspects *seriatim* instead of simultaneously, and partly because the task of scientific research and verification must at some stage lead us to do the same. This is one reason why some of Engels' writings, which have clear exposition as their object, give the impression—by the side of the present essay, for instance—of somewhat over-simplifying or thinning out the density of Marx thought. Some later Marxist expositions, such as Stalin's *Dialectical and Historical Materialism*, have gone much further in this direction; probably too far. Conversely, the wish to emphasise the dialectical unity and interdependence of Marx, may produce merely vague generalisations about dialectics or such observations as that the superstructure is not mechanically or in the short run determined by the base, but reacts back upon it and may from time to time dominate it. Such statements may be of pedagogic value, and serve as warnings against over-simplified views of Marxism (and it is as such that, e.g. Engels, made them in his well-known letter to Bloch), but do not really advance us much farther. There is, as Engels observed to Bloch,[1] one satisfactory way of avoiding these difficulties. It is "to study this theory further from its original sources and not at second-hand". It is for this reason that the present essay, in which the reader may follow Marx *while he is actually thinking*, deserves such close and admiring study.

Most readers will be interested in one major aspect of it: Marx's discussion of the epochs of historic development, which forms the background to the brief

[1] to Joseph Bloch, 21.9.1890.

list given in the Preface to the *Critique of Political
Economy*. This is in itself a complex subject, which
requires us to know something of the development of
Marx and Engels' thinking on history and historical
evolution, and of the fortunes of their main historic
periodisations or divisions in subsequent Marxist
discussion.

The classical formulation of these epochs of human
progress occurs in the Preface to the *Critique of Political
Economy*, of which the *Grundrisse* are a preliminary
draft. There Marx suggested that "in broad outlines
we can designate the Asiatic, the ancient, the feudal
and the modern bourgeois modes of production as so
many epochs in the progress of the economic formation
of society". The analysis which led him to this view,
and the theoretical model of economic evolution which
it implies, are not discussed in the Preface, though
various passages in the *Critique*, and in *Capital*
(especially vol. III) form part of it or are difficult to
understand without it. The *Formen*, on the other hand,
deal almost wholly with this problem. They are
therefore essential reading for anyone who wishes
to understand Marx's ways of thinking in general, or
his approach to the problem of historical evolution and
classification in particular.

This does not mean that we are obliged to accept
Marx's list of historical epochs as given in the Preface,
or in the *Formen*. As we shall see, few parts of Marx's
thought have been more revised by his most devoted
followers than this list—not necessarily with equal
justification—and neither Marx nor Engels rested
content with it for the remainder of their lives. The list,
and a good deal of the discussion in the *Formen* which
lies behind it, are the outcome not of theory but of
observation. The general theory of historical materialism requires only that there should be a succession of
modes of production, though not necessarily any

particular modes, and perhaps not in any particular predetermined order.[1] Looking at the actual historical record, Marx thought that he could distinguish a certain number of socio-economic formations and a certain succession. But if he had been mistaken in his observations, or if these had been based on partial and therefore misleading information, the general theory of historical materialism would remain unaffected. Now it is generally agreed that Marx and Engels' observations on pre-capitalist epochs rest on far less thorough study than Marx's description and analysis of capitalism. Marx concentrated his energies on the study of capitalism, and he dealt with the rest of history in varying degrees of detail, but mainly in so far as it bore on the origins and development of capitalism. Both he and Engels were, so far as history goes, exceptionally well-read laymen, and both their genius and their theory enabled them to make immeasurably better use of their reading than any of their contemporaries. But they relied on such literature as was available to them, and this was far scantier than it is at present. It is therefore useful to survey briefly what Marx and Engels knew of history and what they could not yet know. This does not mean that their knowledge was *insufficient* for the elaboration of their theories of pre-capitalist societies. It may very well have been perfectly adequate. It is an occupational kink of scholars that the mere accumulation of volumes and articles advances understanding. It may merely fill libraries. Nevertheless, a knowledge of the factual basis of Marx's historical analysis is evidently desirable for their understanding.

So far as the history of classical (Greco-Roman) antiquity was concerned, Marx and Engels were almost as well equipped as the modern student who relies on

[1] There are obviously certain limits: it is improbable that a socio-economic formation which rests on, say, a level of technology which requires steam-engines, could occur *before* one which does not.

purely literary sources, though the great bulk of archaeological work and the collection of inscriptions, which have since revolutionised the study of classical antiquity, were not available to them when the *Formen* were written, and neither were the papyri. (Schliemann did not begin his excavations at Troy until 1870 and the first volume of Mommsen's *Corpus Inscriptionum Latinarum* did not appear until 1863.) As classically educated men they had no difficulty in reading Latin and Greek, and we know that they were familiar with even quite recondite sources such as Jornandes, Ammianus Marcellinus, Cassiodorus or Orosius.[1] On the other hand neither a classical education nor the material then available made a serious knowledge of Egypt and the ancient Middle East possible. Marx and Engels did not in fact deal with this region in this period. Even casual references to it are relatively scarce; though this does not mean that Marx and Engels[2] overlooked its historical problems.

In the field of oriental history their situation was rather different. There is no evidence that before 1848 either Marx or Engels thought or read much on this subject. It is probable that they knew no more about oriental history than is contained in Hegel's *Lectures on the Philosophy of History* (which is not illuminating) and such other information as might be familiar to Germans educated in that period. Exile in England, the political developments of the 1850s and above all Marx's economic studies, rapidly transformed their knowledge. Marx himself clearly derived some knowledge of India from the classical economists whom he read or re-read in the early 1850s (J. S. Mill's *Principles*, Adam Smith, Richard Jones's *Introductory Lecture* in 1851).[3] He began to publish articles on China (June 14)and India

---

[1] *Marx und Engels zur Deutschen Geschichte* (Berlin, 1953), I, 88, 616, 49.

[2] Cf. Engels to Marx, May 18, 1853, on the origin of Babylonia; Engels to Marx, June 6, 1853.

[3] Karl Marx, *Chronik Seines Lebens*, 96, 103, 107, 110, 139.

(June 25) for the *New York Daily Tribune* in 1853. It is evident that in this year both he and Engels were deeply preoccupied with the historical problems of the Orient, to the point where Engels attempted to learn Persian.[1] In the early summer of 1853 their correspondence refers to the Rev. C. Foster's *A Historical Geography of Arabia*, Bernier's *Voyages*, Sir William Jones, the orientalist, and parliamentary papers on India, and Stamford Raffles' *History of Java*.[2] It is reasonable to suppose that Marx's views on Asiatic society received their first mature formulation in these months. They were, as will be evident, based on far more than cursory study.

On the other hand Marx's and Engels' study of West European feudalism appears to have proceeded in a different manner. Marx was abreast of current research on medieval agrarian history, which meant in the main the works of Hanssen, Meitzen and Maurer,[3] who are already referred to in *Capital*, vol. I, but in fact there is little sign that at this period he was seriously interested in the problems of the evolution of medieval agriculture or serfdom. (The references are in connection with the actual serfdom of Eastern Europe and especially Rumania.) It was not until *after* publication of *Capital*, vol. I (i.e. also after the substantial drafting of *Capital*, vols. II and III) that this problem evidently began to preoccupy the two friends, notably from 1868, when Marx began seriously to

[1] Engels to Marx, June 6, 1853.
[2] Correspondence May 18-June 14. Among the other oriental sources referred to in Marx's writings between March and December 1853 are G. Campbell, *Modern India* (1852), J. Child's *Treatise on the East India Trade* (1681), J. von Hammer *Geschichte des osmanischen Reiches* (1835), James Mill's *History of India* (1826), Thomas Mun's *A Discourse on Trade, from England into the East Indies* (1621), J. Pollexfen's *England and East India* . . . (1697) and Saltykow; *Lettres sur l'Inde* (1848). He also read and excerpted various other works and parliamentary reports.
[3] G. Hassen, *Die Aufhebung der Leibeigenschaft und die Umgestaltung der gutsherrlich-bäuerlichen Verhältnisse überhaupt in den Herzogthümern Schleswig und Holstein* (St. Petersburg, 1861); G. von Maurer, *Einleitung zur Geschichte der Mark, Hof, Dorf und Stadtverfassung und der öffentlichen Gewalt* (Munich, 1854); *Geschichte der Fronhöfe*, etc., 4 vols. (Erlangen, 1862-3). The *landwirtschaftlichen Verhältnisse des preussischen Staates* (Berlin, 1866).

study Maurer, whose works he and Engels henceforth regarded as the foundation of their knowledge in this field.[1] However, Marx's own interest appears to have lain in the light Maurer and others threw on the original peasant community, rather than on serfdom, though Engels seems from the start to have been interested in this aspect also, and elaborated it on the basis of Maurer in his account of *The Mark* (written 1882). Some of the very last letters exchanged between the two in 1882 deal with the historical evolution of serfdom.[2] It seems clear that Marx's interest in the subject grew towards the end of his life, when the problems of Russia preoccupied him increasingly. The sections of *Capital*, vol. III, which deal with the transformations of rent show no sign of any detailed study of the literature on Western feudal agriculture.

Marx's interest in the medieval origins of the bourgeoisie and in feudal trade and finance was—as is evident from *Capital*, vol. III—very much more intensive. It is clear that he studied not merely general works on the Western Middle Ages, but so far as they were then available, the specialised literature about medieval prices (Thorold Rogers), and medieval banking and currency and medieval trade.[3] Of course the study of these subjects was in its infancy in the period of Marx's most intensive work in the 1850s and 1860s, so that some of his sources both on agrarian and commercial history must be regarded as long obsolete.[4]

In general, Engels' interest in the Western, and especially the Germanic, Middle Ages, was much livelier than Marx's. He read a great deal, including

[1] Marx to Engels, March 14, 1868; Engels to Marx, March 25, 1868; Marx to Vera Zasulich, March 8, 1881; Engels to Bebel, September 23, 1882.

[2] Engels to Marx, December 15, 1882; Marx to Engels, December 16, 1882.

[3] Thorold Rogers is praised as "the first authentic history of prices" of the period in *Capital* I (Torr edn. 692 n.) K. D. Huellmann, *Städtewesen des Mittelalters* (Bonn, 1826-9) is extensively quoted in *Capital* III.

[4] Such as Huellmann, Vincard *Histoire du Travail . . . en France* (1845) or Kindlinger, *Geschichte der deutschen Hörigkeit* (1818).

primary sources and local monographs, drafted outlines of early German and Irish history, was keenly
aware of the importance not only of linguistic evidence
but of archaeology (especially the Scandinavian work
which Marx already noted as outstanding in the 1860s)
and was as keenly aware as any modern scholar of the
crucial importance of such economic documents of the
dark ages as the Polyptych of Abbot Irmino of St.
Germain. However, one cannot escape the impression
that, like Marx, his real interest lay in the ancient
peasant community more than in manorial development.

So far as primitive communal society is concerned,
Marx's and Engels' historic views were almost certainly
transformed by the study of two authors: Georg von
Maurer, who attempted to demonstrate the existence
of communal property as a stage in German history,
and above all Lewis Morgan, whose *Ancient Society*
(1877) provided the basis of their analysis of primitive
communalism. Engels' *The Mark* (1882) is based on
the former, and his *Origin of the Family*, *Private
Property and the State* (1884) is heavily, and equally
frankly, indebted to the latter. Maurer's work (which,
as we have seen, began to make its chief impact on the
two friends in 1868) they considered in a sense as a
liberation of scholarship from the romantic medievalism
which reacted against the French Revolution. (Their
own lack of sympathy with such romanticism may explain something of their own relative neglect of Western
feudal history.) To look back beyond the middle ages
to the primitive epochs of human history, as Maurer
did, appeared to be consonant with the socialist
tendency, even though the German scholars who did
so were not socialists.[1] Lewis Morgan, of course, grew
up in a utopian-socialist atmosphere, and clearly outlined the relation between the study of primitive society
and the future. It was therefore only natural that Marx,

[1] Engels to Marx, March 25, 1868.

who encountered his work soon after its publication and immediately noted the similarity of its results with his own, welcomed and used it; as usual acknowledging his debt with the scrupulous scientific honesty which was so characteristic of him as a scholar. A third source which Marx used abundantly in his later years was the very full literature of Russian scholarship, especially the work of M. M. Kovalevsky.

At the time the *Formen* were written, Marx's and Engels' knowledge of primitive society was therefore only sketchy. It was not based on any serious knowledge of tribal societies, for modern anthropology was in its infancy, and in spite of Prescott's work (which Marx read in 1851 and evidently utilised in the *Formen*) so was our knowledge of pre-Colombian civilisation in the Americas. Until Morgan, most of their views about it were based partly on classical authors, partly on oriental material, but mainly on material from early medieval Europe or the study of communal survivals in Europe. Among these the Slavonic and East European ones played an important part, for the strength of such survivals in those parts had long attracted the attention of scholars. The division into four basic types—oriental (Indian), Greco-Roman, Germanic and Slavonic (cf. p. 95)—fits in with the state of their knowledge in the 1850s.

As for the history of capitalist development, Marx was already a considerable expert by the end of the 1850s, on the basis not so much of the literature of economic history, which then hardly existed, but of the voluminous literature of economic theory, of which he had a profound knowledge. In any case the nature of his knowledge is sufficiently familiar. A glance at the bibliographies attached to most editions of *Capital* will illustrate it. Admittedly by modern standards the information available in the 1850s and 1860s was extremely defective, but we should not for this reason write it off, especially when utilised by a man of Marx's acuteness of mind. Thus it may be argued that our knowledge of the sixteenth-century price-rise and the role of American bullion in it, has only been put on a sound documentary basis since about 1929, or indeed even later. It is easy to forget that at least one basic work on this subject was already available before Marx's death,[1] and even easier to forget that long before this enough was known in general about the subject to permit an intelligent discussion of it, such as that of Marx in the *Critique of Political Economy*.[2] I need hardly add that both Marx and Engels kept abreast of subsequent work in this field.

So much for the general state of Marx and Engels' historical knowledge. We may summarise it as follows. It was (at all events in the period when the *Formen* were drafted) thin on pre-history, on primitive communal societies and on pre-Colombian America, and virtually non-existent on Africa. It was not impressive on the ancient or medieval Middle East, but markedly better on certain parts of Asia, notably India, but not on Japan. It was good on classical antiquity and the European middle ages, though Marx's (and to a lesser extent Engels') interest in this period was uneven. It was, for the times, outstandingly good on the period of rising capitalism. Both men were, of course, close students of history. However, it is probable that there were two periods in Marx's career when he occupied himself more particularly with the history of pre-industrial or non-European societies: the 1850s, i.e. the period which precedes the drafting of the *Critique of Political Economy*, and the 1870s, after the publication of *Capital* I and the substantial drafting of *Capital* II and III, when Marx appears to have reverted

---

[1] A. Soetbeer, *Edelmetall-Produktion und Wertverhältnis zwischen Gold u. Silber seit der Entdeckung Amerikas* . . . (Gotha, 1879), known to Engels.

[2] Marx-Engels, *Werke*, 13 (Berlin, 1961), 135-9, which, incidentally, anticipates the modern critiques of the purely monetary explanation of price-rises.

to historical studies, most notably about Eastern Europe, and primitive society; perhaps in connection with his interest in the possibilities of revolution in Russia.

II

Let us next follow the evolution of Marx's and Engels' views on historical periodisation and evolution. The first stage of this is best studied from the *German Ideology* of 1845-6, which already accepts (what was of course not in itself new) that various stages in the social division of labour correspond to various forms of property. The first of these was communal, and corresponded to "the undeveloped stage of production where a people sustains itself by hunting, fishing, cattle-raising or at most by farming".[1] At this stage social structure is based on the development and modification of the kinship group and its internal division of labour. This kinship group (the "family") tends to develop within itself not only the distinction between chieftains and the rest, but also slavery, which develops with the increase in population and needs, and the growth of external relations, whether of war or barter. The first main advance of the social division of labour consists of the separation of industrial and commercial from agricultural labour, and therefore leads to the distinction between and opposition of town and country. This in turn leads to the second historic phase of property relations, the 'communal and state property of antiquity'. Marx and Engels see its origins in the formation of cities by the union (by agreement or conquest) of tribal groups, slavery continuing to subsist. Communal city property (including that of the citizens over the city slaves) is the main form of property, but side by side with this private property emerges, though at first subordinate to the communal. With the rise first of mobile, later

[1] *Werke*, III, 22.

and especially of immobile private property, this social order decays, and so does the position of the "free citizens", whose position *vis-à-vis* the slaves was based on their collective status as primitive tribesmen.

By now the social division of labour is already rather elaborate. Not only does the division between town and country exist, and even in time between states representing urban and rural interests, but within the city, the division between industry and overseas trade; and of course, that between free men and slaves. Roman society was the ultimate development of this phase of evolution.[1] Its basis was the city, and it never succeeded in going beyond its limitations.

The third historic form of property "feudal or rank ownership"[2] follows chronologically though in fact the *German Ideology* suggests no logical connection between them, but merely notes the succession and the effect of the mixture of broken-down Roman and conquering tribal (Germanic) institutions. Feudalism appears to be in *alternative* evolution out of primitive communalism, under conditions in which no cities develop, because the density of population over a large region is low. The *size* of the area seems to be of decisive importance, for Marx and Engels suggest that

"feudal development starts on a much more extensive territory, and one prepared by the Roman conquests and the spread of agriculture connected with these".[3]

Under these circumstances the countryside and not the city is the point of departure of social organisation. Once again communal property—which in effect turns into the collective property of the feudal lords as a group, backed by the military organisation of the

---

[1] *Werke*, III, 22-3.
[2] There is no adequate English translation of the adjective *ständisch*, for the medieval word "estate" now risks confusion.
[3] *Werke*, III, 24. For the entire argument, 24-5.

Germanic tribal conquerors—is its basis. But the exploited class in opposition to which the feudal nobility organised its hierarchy, and rallied its armed retainers, was not one of slaves but of serfs. At the same time a parallel division existed in the towns. There the basic form of property was the private labour of individuals, but various factors—the needs of defence, competition and the influence of the surrounding feudal organisation of the countryside—produced an analogous social organisation: the gilds of master craftsmen or merchants, which in time confronted the journeymen and apprentices. *Both* landed property worked by serf labour and small-scale craft work with apprentices and journeymen are at this stage described as the "main form of property" under feudalism (*Haupteigentum*). The division of labour was relatively undeveloped, but expressed chiefly in the sharp separation of various "ranks"—princes, nobles, clergy and peasants in the countryside, masters, journeymen, apprentices and eventually a plebs of day-labourers in the cities. This territorially extensive system required relatively large political units in the interests both of the landed nobility and the cities: the feudal monarchies, which therefore became universal.

The transition from feudalism to capitalism, however, is a product of feudal evolution.[1] It begins in the cities, for the separation of town and country is the fundamental and, from the birth of civilisation to the nineteenth century, constant element in and expression of the social division of labour. Within the cities, which once again arose in the Middle Ages, a division of labour between production and trade developed, where it did not already survive from antiquity. This provided the basis of long-distance trade, and a consequent division of labour (specialisation of production) between different cities. The defence of the burghers

[1] *ibid.*, 50-61.

against the feudalists and the interaction between the cities produced a *class* of burghers out of the burgher-groups of individual towns. "The bourgeoisie itself gradually develops as the conditions for its existence arise, splits into different factions again after the division of labour has taken place, and eventually absorbs all existing possessing classes (while developing the majority of the property-less and a part of the hitherto property-owning classes into a new class, the proletariat), to the degree that all existing property is transformed into commercial or industrial capital." Marx adds the note: "In the first instance it absorbs those branches of labour which belong directly to the state, subsequently all more or less ideological estates."[1]

So long as trade has not become world-wide, and is not based on large-scale industry, the technological advances due to these developments remain insecure. They may, being locally or regionally based, be lost in consequence of barbarian invasions or wars, and local advances need not be generalised. (We note in passing that the *German Ideology* here touches on the important problem of historical decay and regression.) The crucial development in capitalism is therefore that of the world market.

The first consequence of the division of labour between towns is the rise of manufactures independent of the gilds, based (as in the pioneer centres of Italy and Flanders) on foreign trade, or (as in England and France) on the internal market. These rest also on a growing density of the population—notably in the countryside—and a growing concentration of capital inside and outside the gilds. Among these manufacturing occupations, weaving (because it depended on the use of machinery, however crude) proved the most important. The growth of manufactures in turn provided means of escape for feudal peasants, who had

[1] *Werke*, III, 53-4.

hitherto fled into the cities, but had been increasingly excluded from them by gild exclusiveness. The source of this labour was partly the former feudal retainers and armies, partly the population displaced by agricultural improvements and the substitution of pasture for tillage.

With the rise of manufactures nations begin to compete as such, and mercantilism (with its trade wars, tariffs and prohibitions) arises on a national scale. Within the manufactures the relation of capitalist and labourer develops. The vast expansion of trade as the result of the discovery of the Americas and the conquest of the sea-route to India, and the mass import of overseas products, notably bullion, shook both the position of feudal landed property and of the labouring class. The consequent change in class relations, conquest, colonisation "and above all the extension of markets into a world market which now became possible and indeed increasingly took place"[1] opened a new phase in historical development.

We need not follow the argument further at this point, beyond noting that the *German Ideology* records two further periods of development before the triumph of industry, up to the middle of the seventeenth century and thenceforward to the end of the eighteenth, and also suggests that the success of Britain in industrial development was due to the concentration of trade and manufacture in that country during the seventeenth century, which gradually created "a relative world market for the benefit of this country, and thereby a demand for its manufacturing products, which could no longer be satisfied by the hitherto existing forces of industrial production".[2]

This analysis is clearly the foundation of the historical sections of the *Communist Manifesto*. Its historical basis is slender—classical antiquity (mostly

[1] *ibid*, 56-7.   [2] *ibid*, 59.

Roman) and Western and Central Europe. It recognises only three forms of class society: the slave society of antiquity, feudalism and bourgeois society. It seems to suggest the first two as *alternative* routes out of primitive communal society, linked only by the fact that the second established itself on the ruins of the first. No mechanism for the breakdown of the former was outlined, though one is probably implicit in the analysis. Bourgeois society in turn is seen to arise, as it were, in the interstices of feudal society. Its growth is sketched entirely—at least to begin with—as that of and within the cities, whose connection with agrarian feudalism is chiefly that of drawing their original population and its reinforcements from former serfs. There is as yet no serious attempt to discover the sources of the surplus population which is to provide the labour force for towns and manufactures, the remarks about this being too sketchy to bear much analytical weight. It must be regarded as a very rough and provisional hypothesis of historical development, though some of the incidental observations it contains are suggestive and some brilliant.

The stage of Marx's thought represented by the *Formen* is considerably more sophisticated and considered, and it is of course based on far greater and more varied historical studies, this time not confined to Europe. The chief innovation in the table of historical periods is the "Asiatic" or "oriental" system, which is incorporated into the famous Preface to the *Critique of Political Economy*.

Broadly speaking, there are now three or four alternative routes out of the primitive communal system, each representing a form of the social division of labour already existing or implicit within it: the *oriental*, the *ancient*, the *Germanic* (though Marx of course does not confine it to any one people) and a somewhat shadowy *Slavonic* form which is not further discussed, but has affinities with the *oriental* (pp. 88, 97). One important distinction between these is the historically crucial one of systems which resist and those which favour historical evolution. The model of 1845-6 only barely touches on this problem, though as we have seen, Marx's view of historical development was never simply unilinear, nor did he ever regard it as a mere record of progress. Nevertheless, by 1857-8 the discussion is considerably more advanced.

Ignorance of the *Formen* has resulted in the discussion of the oriental system in the past being based chiefly on Marx and Engels' earlier letters and on Marx's articles on India (both 1853),[1] where it is characterised—in line with the views of the earliest foreign observers—by "the absence of property in land". This was thought due to special conditions, requiring exceptional centralisation, e.g. the need for public works and irrigation schemes in areas which could not be otherwise effectively cultivated. However, on further consideration, Marx evidently held that the fundamental characteristic of this system was "the self-sustaining unity of manufacture and agriculture" within the village commune, which thus "contains all the conditions for reproduction and surplus production within itself" (pp. 70, 83, 91), and which therefore resisted disintegration and economic evolution more stubbornly than any other system (p. 83). The theoretical absence of property in "oriental despotism" thus masks the "tribal or communal property" which is its base (pp. 69-71). Such systems may be decentralised or centralised, "more despotic or more democratic" in form, and variously organised. Where such small community-units exist as part of a larger unity, they may devote part of their surplus product to pay "the costs of the (larger) community, i.e. for war,

---

[1] Chiefly Marx to Engels, 2.6.53; Engels to Marx, 6.6.53; Marx to Engels, 14.6.53 and *Werke*.

religious worship, etc.", and for economically necessary operations such as irrigation and the maintenance
of communications, which will thus appear to be done
by the higher community, "the despotic government
suspended above the small communities". However,
this alienation of the surplus product contains the
germs of "seignorial *dominium* in its original sense"
and feudalism (villeinage) may develop out of it.
The "closed" nature of the communal units means
that cities hardly belong into the economy at all,
arising "only where the location is particularly favourable to external trade, or where the ruler and his
satraps exchange their revenue (surplus product) for
labour, which they expend as a labour fund" (p. 71).
The Asiatic system is therefore not yet a class society,
or if it is a class society, then it is the most primitive
form. Marx appears to regard Mexican and Peruvian
societies as belonging to the same genus, as also
certain Celtic societies, though complicated—and
perhaps elaborated—by the conquest of some tribes
or communities by others (pp. 70, 88). We note that
it does not *exclude* further evolution, but only as a
luxury, as it were; only in so far as it can develop on
the surplus given by or extorted from the basic self-
sustaining economic units of the tribe or village.

The second system emerging from primitive society
—"the product of a more dynamic historical life"
(p. 71)—produces the *city*, and through it, the *ancient*
mode, an expansionist, dynamic, changing society
(pp. 71-7 and *passim*). "The city with its attached
territory (Landmark) formed the economic whole"
(p. 79). In its developed form—but Marx is careful to
insist on the long process which precedes it, as well as
on . its complexity—it is characterised by chattel-
slavery. But this in turn has its economic limitations,
and had to be replaced by a more flexible and
productive form of exploitation, that of dependent

peasants by lords, *feudalism*, which in turn gives way to *capitalism*.

A third type has as its basic unit neither the village community nor the city, but "each separate household, which forms an independent centre of production (manufacture merely the domestic subsidiary labour of women, etc.)" (p. 79). These separate households are more or less loosely linked with one another (provided they belong to the same tribe) and occasionally unite "for war, religion, the settlement of legal disputes, etc." (p. 80), or for the use—by the individually self-sufficient households—of communal pastures, hunting territory, etc. The basic unit is thus weaker and potentially more "individualist" than the village community. This Marx calls the *Germanic* type, though, we repeat, he clearly does not confine it to any one people.[1] Since the *ancient* and the *Germanic* types are distinguished from the *oriental* type, we may infer that Marx regarded the *Germanic* type in its way as also more potentially dynamic than the oriental, and this is indeed not unlikely.[2] Marx's observations on this type are tantalisingly sketchy, but we know that he and Engels left the way open for a direct transition from primitive society to feudalism, as among the Germanic tribes.

The division between town and country (or agricultural and non-agricultural production) which was fundamental to Marx's analysis in 1845-6 thus remains fundamental in the *Formen*, but it is both more broadly based and more elegantly formulated:

"Ancient history is the history of cities, but of cities founded on agriculture and landed property; Asian

---

[1] The disappearance of this name may be due to the fact that subsequent studies of the specialist literature led Marx to doubt whether his earlier picture of Germanic society had been accurate.

[2] Cf. G. C. Homans, "The Rural Sociology of Medieval England", *Past and Present*, 4, 1953, for the different tendencies of development of communal and single-family settlements.

history is a kind of undifferentiated unity of town and country (the large city, properly speaking, must be regarded merely as a princely camp superimposed on the real economic structure); the Middle Ages (Germanic period) starts with the countryside as the location of history, whose further development then proceeds by the opposition of town and country; modern history is the urbanisation of the country-side, not, as among the ancients, the ruralisation of the city" (pp. 77-8).

However, while these different forms of the social division of labour are clearly alternative forms of the break-up of communal society, they are apparently presented—in the Preface to the *Critique of Political Economy*, though not specifically in the *Formen*—as *successive* historical stages. In the literal sense this is plainly untrue, for not only did the Asiatic mode of production co-exist with all the rest, but there is no suggestion in the argument of the *Formen*, or anywhere else, that the ancient mode evolved out of it. We ought therefore to understand Marx not as referring to chronological succession, or even to the evolution of one system out of its predecessor (though this is obviously the case with capitalism and feudalism), but to evolution in a more general sense. As we saw earlier, "Man only becomes an individual (*vereinzelt sich selbst*) by means of the historical process. He appears originally as a generic being, a tribal being, a herd animal." The different forms of this gradual individualisation of man, which means the break-up of the original unity, correspond to the different stages of history. Each of these represents, as it were, a step away from "the original unity of a specific form of (tribal) community and the property in nature connected with it, or the relation to the objective conditions of production as naturally existing (*Naturdaseins*)" (p. 94). They represent, in other words, steps in the evolution of private property.

Marx distinguishes four analytical, though not chronological, stages in this evolution. The first is direct communal property, as in the oriental, and in a modified form the slavonic system, neither of which, it would seem, can as yet be regarded as fully formed class societies. The second is communal property continuing as the substratum of what is already a "contradictory", i.e. class, system, as in the ancient and the Germanic forms. The third stage arises, if we are to follow Marx's argument, not so much through feudalism as through the rise of *crafts* manufacture, in which the independent craftsman (organised corporatively in gilds) already represents a far more individual form of the control over the means of production, and indeed of consumption, which allow him to live while he produces. It would seem that what Marx has in mind here is a certain autonomy of the craft sector of production, for he deliberately excludes the manufactures of the ancient orient, though without giving reasons. The fourth stage is that in which the proletarian arises; that is to say in which exploitation is no longer conducted in the crude form of the appropriation of *men*—as slaves or serfs—but in the appropriation of "labour". "For Capital the worker does not constitute a condition of production, but only labour. If this can be performed by machinery, or even by water or air, so much the better. And what capital appropriates is not the labourer but his labour—and not directly, but by means of exchange" (p. 99).

It would seem—though in view of the difficulty of Marx's thought and the elliptical quality of his notes one cannot be sure—that this analysis fits into a schema of the historical stages in the following way. The oriental (and Slavonic) forms are historically closest to man's origins, since they conserve the

functioning primitive (village) community in the midst
of the more elaborate social superstructure, and have
an insufficiently developed class system. (Of course, we
may add, that at the time Marx was writing he observed that both these systems were disintegrating
under the impact of the world market and their special
character was therefore disappearing.) The ancient
and Germanic systems, though also primary—i.e. not
derived from the oriental—represent a somewhat more
articulated form of evolution out of primitive communalism; but the "Germanic system" as such does
not form a special socio-economic formation. It forms the
socio-economic formation of feudalism in conjunction
with the medieval town (the locus of the emergence of
the autonomous craft production). This combination
then, which emerges during the Middle Ages, forms
the third phase. Bourgeois society, emerging out of
feudalism, forms the fourth. The statement that the
Asiatic, ancient, feudal and bourgeois formations are
"progressive" does not therefore imply any simple
unilinear view of history, not a simple view that all
history is progress. It merely states that each of these
systems is in crucial respects further removed from the
primitive state of man.

III

The next point to be considered is the internal
dynamic of these systems: what makes them rise and
decline? This is relatively simple for the oriental
system, whose characteristics make it resistant to
disintegration and economic evolution, until wrecked
by the external force of capitalism. Marx tells us too
little about the slavonic system at this stage to permit
much comment. On the other hand his views of the
internal contradiction of the ancient and feudal system
are complex, and raise some difficult problems.

Slavery is the chief characteristic of the ancient

system, but Marx's views on its basic internal contradiction is more complex than the simple view that slavery imposes limits to further economic evolution and thus produces its own breakdown. It should be noted in passing that the basis of his analysis appears to be the West Roman rather than the Greek half of the Mediterranean. Rome begins as a community of peasants, though its organisation is urban. Ancient history is "a history of cities founded on landed property and agriculture" (p. 77). It is not an entirely equal community, for tribal developments combined with intermarriages and conquests already tend to produce socially higher and lower kin groups, but the Roman citizen is essentially a landowner, and "the continuation of the commune is the reproduction of all its members as self-sustaining peasants, whose surplus time belongs precisely to the commune, the (communal) labour of war, etc." (p. 74). For war is its primary business, because the only threat to its existence comes from other communities which seek its land, and the only way to secure each citizen land as population expands, is to occupy it by force (p. 71). But the very warlike and expansive tendencies of such peasant communities must lead to the break-up of the peasant qualities which are its basis. Up to a point slavery, the concentration of landed property, exchange, a monetary economy, conquest, etc., are compatible with the foundations of this community. Beyond this point it must lead to its breakdown, and must make the evolution of society or of the individual impossible (pp. 83-4). Even *before* the development of a slave economy, therefore, the ancient form of social organisation is crucially limited, as is indicated by the fact that with it the development of productivity is not and cannot be a fundamental preoccupation. "Among the ancients we never encounter an enquiry into which forms of landed property, etc., are the most productive, create maximum wealth. . . . The enquiry is always about which kind of property creates the best citizen. Wealth as an end in itself appears only among a few trading peoples—monopolists of the carrying trade—who live in the pores of the ancient world like the Jews in medieval society" (p. 84).

Two major factors therefore tend to undermine it. The first is the social differentiation within the community, against which the peculiar ancient combination of communal and private landed property provides no safeguard. It is possible for the individual citizen to *lose* his property—i.e. the basis of his citizenship. The more rapid the economic development, the more is this likely: hence the ancient suspicion of trade and manufacture, which are best left to freedmen, clients or foreigners, and their belief in the dangers of intercourse with foreigners, desire to exchange surplus products, etc. Second, of course, there is slavery. For the very necessity to restrict citizenship (or what amounts to the same thing, landed property) to members of the conquering community leads naturally to the enslavement or enserfment of the conquered. "Slavery and serfdom are therefore simply further developments of property based on tribalism" (p. 91). Hence "the preservation of the community implies the destruction of the conditions on which it rests, and turns into its opposite" (p. 93). The "commonwealth", first represented by all citizens, is represented by the aristocratic patricians, who remain the only ones to be full landowners against the lesser men and the slaves and by the citizens against the non-citizens and slaves. The actual economic contradictions of a slave economy are not discussed by Marx in this context at all. At the very general level of his analysis in the *Formen*, they are merely a special aspect of the fundamental contradiction of ancient society. Nor does he here discuss why in antiquity it was slavery rather than serfdom which developed. One may conjecture that it was because of the level of productive forces and the complexity of the social relations of production already reached in the ancient Mediterranean.

The breakdown of the ancient mode is therefore implicit in its socio-economic character. There seems to be no logical reason why it must lead *inevitably* to feudalism, as distinct from other "new forms, combinations of labour" (p. 93) which would make higher productivity possible. On the other hand a direct transition from the ancient mode to capitalism is excluded.

When we come to feudalism, out of which capitalism *did* develop, the problem becomes very much more puzzling, if only because Marx tells us so little about it. No sketch of the internal contradictions of feudalism, comparable to that of the ancient mode, is to be found in the *Formen*. Nor is there ever any real discussion of serfdom (any more than of slavery). Indeed these two relations of production often appear bracketed together, sometimes as "the relation of domination and subordination", in contrast to the position of the free labourer.[1] The element within feudal society from which capitalism derives appears to be, in 1857-8 as in 1845-6, the *city*—more specifically the city merchants and craftsmen (cf. pp. 97-8, 100). It is the emancipation of ownership in the means of production from its communal basis, such as occurs among the medieval crafts, which provides the basis of the separation of "labour" from the "objective conditions of production". It is the same development—the formation of the 'working owner' by the side of and outside landed property—the craft and urban evolution of labour—which is "not ... an aspect (*Akzident*) of landed property and subsumed under it" (p. 100), which

---

[1] As, e.g., in pp. 87, 89, 99. The usage in *Capital* III is also in general of this sort, e.g. (Berlin, 1956 edn.) 357, 665, 684, 873, 885, 886, 937.

provides the basis of the evolution of the capitalist. The role of agricultural feudalism in this process is not discussed, but would seem to be rather negative. It must, at the right moment, make it possible for the peasant to be separated from the soil, the retainer from his lord, in order to turn him into a wage-labourer. Whether this takes the form of the dissolution of villeinage (*Hörigkeit*), of the private property or possession of yeomen or peasant tenants, or of various forms of clientship, is irrelevant. The important thing is that none of these should stand in the way of the transformation of men into at least potentially free labour.

However, though this is not discussed in the *Formen* (but in *Capital* III) serfdom and other analogous relations of dependence differ from slavery in economically significant ways. The serf, though under the control of the lord, is in fact an economically independent producer; the slave is not.[1] Take away lords from serfdom and what is left is small commodity production; separate plantations and slaves and (until the slaves do something else) no kind of economy is left. "Hence what is required are conditions of personal dependence, personal unfreedom in whatever form, the attachment of men as an adjunct to the land, villeinage in the proper sense of the word" (*Capital* III, 841). For under conditions of serfdom the serf produces not merely the labour surplus which his lord, in one form or another, appropriates, but he can also accumulate a profit for himself. Since, for various reasons, in economically primitive and undeveloped systems such as feudalism there is a tendency for the surplus to remain unchanged as a conventional magnitude, and since "the use of (the serf's) labour power is by no means confined to agriculture, but includes rural domestic manufactures. There is here

[1] *Capital*, III, 841.

the possibility of a certain economic evolution . . ." (*Capital*, III, 844-5).

Marx discusses these aspects of serfdom no more than the internal contradictions of slavery, because in the *Formen* it is not his business to outline an "economic history" of either. Indeed, as elsewhere—though here in a rather more general form—he is not concerned with the internal dynamics of pre-capitalist systems except in so far as they explain the preconditions of capitalism.[1] Here he is interested merely in two negative questions: why could "labour" and "capital" not arise out of pre-capitalist socio-economic formations other than feudalism? and why did feudalism in its agrarian form allow them to emerge, and not impose fundamental obstacles to their emergence?

This explains obvious gaps in his treatment. As in 1845-6, there is no discussion of the specific *modus operandi* of feudal agriculture. There is no discussion of the specific relationship between the feudal city and countryside, or why the one should produce the other. On the other hand there is the implication that European feudalism is *unique*, for no other form of this system produced the medieval city, which is crucial to the Marxian theory of the evolution of capitalism. In so far as feudalism is a general mode of production existing outside Europe (or perhaps Japan, which Marx nowhere discusses in detail), there is nothing in Marx to authorise us to look for some "general law" of development which might explain its tendency to evolve into capitalism.

What *is* discussed in the *Formen* is the "Germanic system", i.e. a particular sub-variety of primitive communalism, which therefore tends to evolve a particular type of social structure. Its crux, as we have seen, seems to be scattered settlement in economically

[1] Even in *Capital* III, where he discusses the subject of feudal agriculture most fully, he specifically disclaims the intention of analysing landed property in its differing historical forms. Cf. cap. 37, p. 662, and again 842.

self-sustaining family units, as against the peasant city of the ancients: "Every individual household contains an entire economy, forming as it does an independent centre of production (manufacture merely the domestic subsidiary labour of the women, etc.). In the ancient world the city with its attached territory (*Landmark*) formed the economic whole, in the Germanic world it is the individual homestead" (p. 79). Its existence is safeguarded by its bond with other similar homesteads belonging to the same tribe, a bond expressed in the occasional assembly of all homesteaders for the purpose of war, religion, settlement of disputes, and in general for mutual security (p. 80). In so far as there is common property, as in pastures, hunting grounds, etc., it is used by each member as an individual, and not as in ancient society, as a representative of the commonwealth. One might compare the ideal of Roman social organisation to an Oxford or Cambridge college, whose fellows are co-possessors of land and buildings only in so far as they form a body of fellows, but who cannot, as individuals, be said to "own" it or any part of it. The Germanic system might then be comparable to a housing co-operative in which the individual occupation of a man's flat depends on his union and continued co-operation with other members, but in which nevertheless individual possession exists in an identifiable form. This looser form of community, which implies a greater potentiality of economic individualisation, makes the "Germanic system" (via feudalism) the direct ancestor of bourgeois society.

How this system evolves into feudalism is not discussed, though various possibilities of internal and external social differentiation (e.g. by the effect of war and conquest) present themselves. One may hazard the guess that Marx attached considerable importance to military organisation (since war is, in the Germanic as in the ancient system, "one of the earliest tasks of all such primitive (*naturwüchsig*) communities, both for the preservation and the acquisition of its property)" (p. 89). This is certainly the later line of explanation in Engels' *Origin of the Family*, where kingship arises out of the transformation of gentile military leadership among the Teutonic tribes. There is no reason for supposing that Marx would have thought differently. What were the internal contradictions of feudalism? How did it evolve into capitalism? These problems have increasingly preoccupied Marxist historians, as in the vigorous international discussion arising out of M. H. Dobb's *Studies in the Development of Capitalism* in the early 1950s and the slightly subsequent debate on the "fundamental economic law of feudalism" in the U.S.S.R. Whatever the merits of either discussion —and those of the first appear to be rather greater than those of the second—both of them are evidently handicapped by the absence of any indication of Marx's own views on the subject. It is not impossible that Marx might have agreed with Dobb that the cause of feudal decline was "the inefficiency of Feudalism as a system of production, coupled with the growing needs of the ruling class for revenue" (*Studies*, 42), though Marx appears, if anything, to stress the relative inflexibility of the demands of the feudal ruling class, and its tendency to fix them conventionally.[1] It is equally possible that he would have approved of R. H. Hilton's view that "the struggle for rent was the 'prime mover' in feudal society" (*Transition*, 70), though he would almost certainly have rejected as over-simplified Porshnev's view that the simple struggle of the exploited masses was such a prime mover. But the point is that Marx nowhere appears to anticipate any of these lines of argument; certainly not in the *Formen*.

[1] *Capital* III, 843-5 (chapter 47, sect. II).

If any of the participants in these discussions can be said to follow his identifiable trails, it is P. M. Sweezy, who argues (following Marx) that feudalism is a system of production for use,[1] and that in such economic formations "no boundless thirst for surplus labour arises from the nature of production itself" (*Capital* I, 219, ch. x, section 2). Hence the main agent of disintegration was the growth of trade, operating more particularly through the effects of the conflict and interplay between a feudal countryside and the towns which developed on its margin (*Transition*, 2, 7-12). This line of argument is very similar to that of the *Formen*.

For Marx the conjunction of three phenomena is necessary to account for the development of capitalism out of feudalism: first, as we have seen, a rural social structure which allows the peasantry to be "set free" at a certain point; second, the urban craft development which produces specialised, independent, non-agricultural commodity production in the form of the crafts; and third, accumulations of monetary wealth derived from trade and usury (Marx is categorical on this last point (pp. 107-8)). The formation of such monetary accumulations "belongs to the pre-history of bourgeois economy" (p. 113); nor are they as yet capital. Their mere existence, or even their apparent predominance, do not automatically produce capitalist development, otherwise "ancient Rome, Byzantium, etc., would have ended their history with free labour and capital" (p. 109). But they are essential.

Equally essential is the urban craft element. Marx's observations on this are elliptic and allusive, but its importance in his analysis is clear. It is above all the element of craft skill, pride and organisation which he

---

[1] This is not widely denied by Marxists, though it must not be confused with the statement that systems of the production of use-values are also sometimes systems of natural economy.

stresses.[1] The main importance of the formation of the medieval craft appears to be that, by developing "labour itself as skill determined by craft [it becomes] a property itself, and not mere the source of property" (p. 104), and thus introduces a potential separation between làbour and the other conditions of production, which expresses a higher degree of individualisation than the communal and makes possible the formation of the category of free labour. At the same time it develops special skills and their instruments. But in the craft-gild stage "the instrument of labour is still so intimately merged with living labour, that it does not truly circulate" (p. 108). And yet, though it cannot *by itself* produce the labour market, the development of exchange production and money can only create the labour market "under the precondition of urban *craft activity*, which rests *not* on capital and wage labour but on the organisation of labour in gilds, etc." (p. 112).

But all these also require the potentially soluble rural structure. For capitalism cannot develop without "the involvement of the entire countryside in the production not of use—but of exchange-values" (p. 116). This is another reason why the ancients, who, while contemptuous and suspicious of the crafts, had produced a version of "urban craft activity", could not produce large-scale industry (*ibid.*). What precisely makes the rural structure of feudalism thus soluble, apart from the characteristics of the "Germanic system" which is its substratum, we are not told. And indeed, in the context of Marx's argument at this point, it is not necessary to probe further. A number of effects of the growth of an exchange-economy are mentioned in passing (e.g. p. 112-13). It is also noted that "in part this process of separation [of labour from the objective

---

[1] Words such as *würdiges Zunftwesen* ("the dignity of the gild system)", p. 76, "labour as half artistic, half performed for its own sake" (p. 98) *städitscher Gewerbefleiss* ("urban craft activity", p. 112) are constantly used. All carry emotional, and indeed in general approving overtones.

conditions of production—food, raw materials, instruments] took place without [monetary wealth]" (p. 113). The nearest thing to a general account (pp. 114 ff.) implies that capital first appears sporadically or *locally* (Marx's emphasis) *by the side* (Marx's emphasis) of the old modes of production, but subsequently breaks them up everywhere.

Manufacture for the foreign market arises first on the basis of long-distance trade and in the centres of such trade, not in the gild-crafts, but in the least skilled and gild-controlled rural supplementary trades such as spinning and weaving, though also of course in such urban branches directly connected with shipping as shipbuilding. On the other hand in the countryside the peasant tenant appears, as does the transformation of the rural population into free day-labourers. All these manufactures require the pre-existence of a mass market. The dissolution of serfdom and the rise of manufactures gradually transform all branches of production into capitalist ones, while in the cities a class of day-labourers, etc., outside the gilds provides an element in the creation of a proper proletariat (p. 114-17).[1]

The destruction of the rural supplementary trades creates an *internal* market for capital based on the substitution of manufacture or industrial production for the former rural supply of consumer goods. "This process arises automatically (*von selbst*) from the separation of the labourers from the soil and from their property (though even only serf property) in the conditions of production" (p. 118). The transformation of urban crafts into industry proceeds later, for it requires a considerable advance of productive methods in order to be capable of factory production. At this point Marx's manuscript, which deals specifically with

---

[1] Marx here underestimates the differentiation of urban crafts into virtual employers and virtual wage-labourers.

pre-capitalist formations, ends. The phases of capitalist development are not discussed.

IV

We must next consider how far Marx's and Engel's subsequent thinking and study led them to modify, amplify and follow up the general views expressed in the *Formen*. This was notably the case in the field of the study of primitive communalism. It is certain that Marx's own historical interests after the publication of *Capital* (1867) were overwhelmingly concerned with this stage of social development, for which Maurer, Morgan, and the ample Russian literature which he devoured from 1873 on, provided a far more solid base of study than had been available in 1857-8. Apart from the agrarian orientation of his work in *Capital* III, two reasons for this concentration of interests may be suggested. First, the development of a Russian revolutionary movement increasingly led Marx and Engels to place their hopes for a European revolution in Russia. (No misinterpretation of Marx is more grotesque than the one which suggests that he expected a revolution exclusively from the advanced industrial countries of the West.[1]) Since the position of the village community was a matter of fundamental theoretical disagreement among Russian revolutionaries, who consulted Marx on the point, it was natural for him to investigate the subject at greater length.

It is interesting, that—somewhat unexpectedly— his views inclined towards those of the Narodniks, who believed that the Russian village community could

[1] Engels records their hopes of a Russian revolution in the late 1870s, and in 1894 specifically looks forward to the possibility of "the Russian revolution giving the signal for the workers' revolution in the West, so that both supplement each other". *Werke*, XVIII, 668. For other references: Marx to Sorge, 27.9.1877; Engels to Bernstein, 22.2.1882.

provide the basis of a transition to socialism without prior disintegration through capitalist development. This view does not follow from the natural trend of Marx's earlier historical thought, was not accepted by the Russian Marxists (who were among the Narodniks' opponents on this point) or by subsequent Marxists, and in any case proved to be unfounded. Perhaps the difficulty Marx had in drafting a theoretical justification of it,[1] reflects a certain feeling of awkwardness. It contrasts strikingly with Engels' lucid and brilliant return to the main Marxist tradition—and to support for the Russian Marxists—when discussing the same topic some years later.[2] Nevertheless, it may lead us to the second reason for Marx's increasing preoccupation with primitive communalism: his growing hatred of and contempt for capitalist society. (The view that the older Marx lost some of the revolutionary ardour of the younger, is always popular among critics who wish to abandon the revolutionary practice of Marxism while retaining a fondness for his theory.) It seems probable that Marx, who had earlier welcomed the impact of Western capitalism as an inhuman but historically progressive force on the stagnant pre-capitalist economies, found himself increasingly appalled by this inhumanity. We know that he had always admired the positive social values embodied, in however backward a form, in the primitive community. And it is certain that after 1857-8—both in *Capital* III[3] and in the subsequent Russian discussions[4]—he increasingly stressed the viability of the primitive commune, its powers of resistance to historical disintegration and even—though perhaps only in the context of the Narodnik discussion—its capacity to develop into a higher form of economy without prior

[1] In a letter to Vera Zasulich, 1881. Four drafts of this letter—three of them printed in *Werke*, XIX, 384-406—survive.
[2] Nachwort (1894) zu "Soziales aus Russland" (*Werke*, XVIII, 663-4).
[3] *Capital*, III, 365-6.   [4] e.g. drafts to Zasulich, *loc. cit.*, 387, 388, 402, 404.

destruction.[1] This is not the place to give a detailed account of Marx's outline of primitive evolution in general, as available in Engels' *Origin of the Family*[2] and on the agrarian community in particular. However, two general observations about this body of work are relevant here. First, pre-class society forms a large and complex historical epoch of its own, with its own history and laws of development, and its own varieties of socio-economic organisation, which Marx tends now to call collectively "the archaic Formation" or "Type".[3] This, it seems clear, includes the four basic variants of primitive communalism, as set out in the *Formen*. It probably also includes the "Asiatic mode" (which we have seen to be the most primitive of the developed socio-economic formations), and may explain why this mode apparently disappears from Engels' systematic treatments of the subject in *Anti-Dühring* and *Origin of the Family*.[4] It is possible that Marx and Engels also had in mind some sort of intermediate historical phase

[1] G. Lichtheim (*loc. cit.*, 98) is right to draw attention to this growing hostility to capitalism and fondness for surviving primitive communities, but wrong to suggest that the Marx of 1858 had seen these in an entirely negative light. That communism would be a recreation, on a higher level, of the social virtues of primitive communalism, is an idea that belongs to the earliest heritage of socialism. "Genius," said Fourier, "must discover the paths of that primitive happiness and adapt it to the conditions of modern indutry" (quoted in J. Talmon, *Political Messianism*, London, 1960). p. 127. For the views of the early Marx, cf. *Das philosophische Manifest der historischen Rechtsschule*, of 1842 (*Werke*, I, 78): "A current fiction of the eighteenth century saw the state of nature as the true state of human nature. Men desired to see the Idea of Man with their very own eyes, and therefore created 'natural men', Papagenos, whose very feathered skin expressed their naïvety. In the last decades of the eighteenth century the primitive peoples were suspected of original wisdom, and birdcatchers could be overheard everywhere imitating the song of the Iroquois or the Indian, in the belief that by these means the birds themselves might be captured. All such eccentricities rested on the correct idea, that *crude* conditions are naïve paintings, as it were in the Dutch manner, of *true* conditions." Cf. also Marx to Engels, 25.3.1868, on Maurer's contribution to history.
[2] This was a work which Marx wanted to write, and for which he had prepared voluminous notes, on which Engels based himself so far as possible. Cf. Preface to First Edition, 1884 (*Werke*, XXI, 27).
[3] Drafts to Vera Zasulich, *loc. cit.*, *passim*.
[4] "Slavery is the *first* (my emphasis—E.J.H.) form of exploitation, and belongs to antiquity; it is followed by serfdom in the Middle Ages, by wage-labour in modern times. These are the three great forms of servitude, characteristic of the three great epochs of civilisation" (*Origin*, in *Werke*, XXI, 170). It is evident from this text that no attempt is here made to include what Marx called the "Asiatic" mode under any of the three heads listed. It is omitted, as belonging to the pre-history of "civilisation".

of communal disintegration, out of which ruling classes of different types might emerge.

Second, the analysis of "archaic" social evolution is in every way consistent with the analysis sketched in the *German Ideology* and the *Formen*. It merely elaborates them, as when the brief references to the crucial importance of human (sexual) reproduction and the family in the *Ideology*[1] are expanded, in the light of Morgan, into the *Origin of the Family*, or when the summary analysis of primitive communal property is filled out and modified (in the light of scholars like Kovalevsky, who, incidentally, was himself influenced by Marx), into the stages of disintegration of the agrarian community of the Zasulich drafts.

A second field in which the founders of Marxism continued their special studies was that of the feudal period. This was Engels' rather than Marx's favourite.[2] A good deal of his work, dealing as it did with the origins of feudalism, overlaps with Marx's studies of primitive communal forms. Nevertheless, Engels' interests appear to have been slightly different from Marx's. He was probably preoccupied rather less with the survival or disintegration of the primitive community, and rather more with the rise and decline of feudalism. His interest in the dynamics of serf agriculture was more marked that Marx's. In so far as we possess analyses of these problems from the later years of Marx's lifetime, they are in Engels' formulation. Moreover, the political and military element plays a rather prominent part in Engels' work. Lastly, he concentrated almost entirely on medieval Germany (with an excursus or two on Ireland, with which had he personal connections), and was undoubtedly more

---

[1] *Werke*, III, 29-30.

[2] *Anti-Dühring, Origin of the Family*, the little essay on *The Mark*, and *The German Peasant War* are the chief published works, but drafts and notes (mostly incomplete) exist about medieval German and Irish history. Cf. *Werke*, XVI, 459-500; XIX, 425-521; XXI, 392-401.

preoccupied than Marx with the rise of nationality and
its function in historic development. Some of these
differences in emphasis are due merely to the fact that
Engels' analysis operates on a less general level than
Marx's; which is one reason why it is often more
accessible and stimulating to those who make their
first acquaintance with Marxism. Some of them are
not. However, while recognising both that the two
men were not Siamese twins and that (as Engels
recognised) Marx was much the greater thinker, we
should beware of the modern tendency of contrasting
Marx and Engels, generally to the latter's disadvan-
tage. When two men collaborate as closely as Marx and
Engels did over forty years, without any theoretical
disagreement of substance, it is to be presumed that
they know what is in each other's minds. Doubtless if
Marx had written *Anti-Dühring* (published in his lifetime) it would have read differently, and perhaps
contained some new and profound suggestions. But
there is no reason at all to believe that he disagreed
with its content. This also applies to the works Engels
wrote after Marx's death.

Engels' analysis of feudal development (which is
seen exclusively in European terms) attempts to fill
several of the gaps left in the extremely global analysis
of 1857-8. In the first place a logical connection
between the decline of the ancient and the rise of the
feudal mode is established, in spite of the fact that one
was established by foreign barbarian invaders on the
ruins of the other. In ancient times the only possible
form of large-scale agriculture was that of the slave
latifundium, but beyond a certain point this had to
become uneconomic, and give way once again to small-
scale agriculture as "the only profitable (*lohnende*)
form".[1] Hence ancient agriculture was already halfway
towards medieval. Small-scale cultivation was the

---

[1] *Origin of the Family, Werke*, XXI, 144.

dominant form in feudal agriculture, it being "operationally" irrelevant that some of the peasantry were free, some owed various obligations to lords. The same type of small-scale production by petty owners of their own means of production predominated in the cities.[1] Though this was under the circumstances a more economic form of production, the general backwardness of economic life in the early feudal period—the predominance of local self-sufficiency, which left scope for the sale or diversion of only a marginal surplus—imposed its limitations. While it guaranteed that any system of lordship (which was necessarily based on one of the control of large estates or bodies of their cultivators) must "necessarily produce large ruling landowners and dependent petty peasants", it also made it impossible to exploit such large estates either by the ancient methods of slavery or by modern large-scale serf agriculture; as proved by the failure of Charlemagne's imperial "villas". The only exception were the monasteries, which were "abnormal social bodies", being founded on celibacy, and consequently their exceptional economic performance must remain exceptional.[2]

While this analysis plainly somewhat underestimates the role of large-scale lay demesne agriculture in the high middle ages, it is exceedingly acute, especially in its distinction between the large estate as a social, political and fiscal unit, and as a unit of *production*, and in its emphasis on the predominance of peasant agriculture rather than demesne agriculture in feudalism. However, it leaves the origin of villeinage and feudal lorship somewhat in the air. Engels' own explanation of it appears to be social, political and military rather than economic. The free Teutonic peasantry was impoverished by constant war, and (given the weakness of royal power) had to place itself

---

[1] *Anti-Dühring, Werke,* XX, 164, 220, 618.   [2] *Origin of Family, loc. cit.,* 148-9.

under the protection of nobles or clergy.[1] At bottom this is due to the inability of a form of social organisation based on kinship to administer or control the large political structures created by its successful conquests: these therefore automatically implied both the origin of classes and of a state.[2] In its simple formulation this hypothesis is not very satisfactory, but the derivation of class origins from the contradictions of social structure (and not simply from a primitive economic determinism) is important. It continues the line of thought of the 1857-8 manuscripts, e.g. on slavery.

The decline of feudalism depends, once again, on the rise of crafts and trade, and the division and conflict between town and country. In terms of agrarian development it expressed itself in an increase in the feudal lords' demand for consumer goods (and arms or equipment) available only by purchase.[3] Up to a point —given stagnant technical conditions of agriculture— an increase in the surplus extracted from the peasants could be achieved only extensively—e.g. by bringing new land under cultivation, founding new villages. But this implied "friendly agreement with the colonists, whether villeins or free men". Hence—and also because the primitive form of lordship contained no incentive to intensify exploitation, but rather a tendency for fixed peasant burdens to become lighter as time went on—peasant freedom tended to increase markedly, especially after the thirteenth century. (Here again Engels' natural ignorance of the development of demesne market agriculture in the high middle ages and the "feudal crisis" of the fourteenth century somewhat over-simplifies and distorts his picture.)

But from the fifteenth century the opposite tendency prevailed, and lords reconverted free men into serfdom,

---

[1] ibid., 146-8.   [2] ibid., 146, 164. The Mark (Werke, XIX, 324-5).
[3] The Mark, loc. cit., 326-7. On the need for urban-made arms, Engels' draft Über den Verfall des Feudalismus und das Aufkommen der Bourgeoisie (Werke, XXI, 392).

and turned peasant land into their own estates. This was (in Germany at least) due not merely to the growing demands of the lords, which could henceforth be met only by growing sales from their own estates, but by the growing power of the princes, which deprived the nobility of other former sources of income such as highway robbery and other similar extortions.[1] Hence feudalism ends with a revival of large-scale agriculture on the basis of serfdom, and peasant expropriation corresponding to—and derived from—the growth of capitalism. "The capitalist era in the countryside is ushered in by a period of large-scale agriculture (*landwirtschaftlichen Grossbetriebs*) on the basis of serf labour services."

This picture of the decline of feudalism is not entirely satisfactory, though it marks an important advance in the original Marxist analysis of feudalism —namely, the attempt to establish, and take into account, the dynamics of feudal agriculture, and especially the relations between lords and dependent peasants. This is almost certainly due to Engels, for it is he who (in the letters relating to the composition of *The Mark*) lays special emphasis on the movements of labour services, and indeed points out that Marx was formerly mistaken in this matter.[2] It introduces (on the basis largely of Maurer) the line of analysis in medieval agrarian history which has since proved exceptionally fruitful. On the other hand it is still worth noting that this field of study appears to be marginal to Marx's and Engels' major interests. The writings in which Engels deals with the problem are short and cursory, compared to those in which he deals with the origin of feudal society.[3] The argument is by no means worked out. No adequate or direct explanation is

---

[1] *The Mark, loc. cit.,* 326-7.   [2] Engels to Marx, 15.12.1882, 16.12.1882.
[3] *The Mark*—whose object is only in passing to deal with the movements of feudal agriculture—was intended as an 8-10 page appendix to *Anti-Dühring*, and the unpublished *Ueber den Verfall* as a prefatory note to a new edition of the *Peasant War*.

given why large-scale agriculture, which was uneconomic in the early middle ages, once again became
economic on a serf (or other) basis at their end.
More surprisingly (in view of Engels' keen interest in
the technological developments of the transition from
antiquity to the middle ages, as recorded by archaeology[1]), technological changes in farming are not
really discussed, and there are a number of other loose
ends. No attempt to apply the analysis outside Western
and Central Europe is made, except for a very suggestive remark about the existence of the primitive
agrarian community under the form of direct and
indirect villeinage (*Hörigkeit*), as in Russia and Ireland,[2] and a remark—which seems somewhat in
advance on the rather later discussion in *The Mark*—
that in Eastern Europe the second enserfment of the
peasants was due to the rise of an export market in
agricultural produce and grew in proportion to it.[3]
Altogether it does not seem that Engels had any
intention of altering the general picture of the transition
from feudalism to capitalism which he and Marx had
formulated many years earlier.

No other major excursions into the history of "forms
which precede the capitalist" occur in the last years of
Marx and Engels, though important work on the
period since the sixteenth century, and especially
contemporary history, was done. It therefore remains
only to discuss briefly two aspects of their later thoughts
on the problem of the phases of social development.
How far did they maintain the list of formations as set
out in the Preface to the *Critique of Political Economy?*
What other general factors about socio-economic
development did they consider or reconsider?

As we have seen, in their later years Marx and
Engels tended to distinguish or to imply sub-varieties,

---

[1] Cf. *Zur Urgeschichte der Deutschen, Werke*, XIX, esp. 450-60.
[2] *Anti-Dühring*: preparatory notes (*Werke*, XX, 587-8). [3] *ibid.*, 588.

sub-phases and transitional forms within their larger social classifications, and notably within pre-class society. But no major changes in the general list of formations occur, unless we count the almost formal transfer of the "Asiatic mode" to the "archaic type" of society. There is—at least on Marx's part—no inclination to abandon the Asiatic mode (and even a tendency to rehabilitate the "Slavonic" mode); and quite certainly a deliberate refusal to reclassify it as feudal. Arguing against Kovalevsky's view that three of the four main criteria of Germano-Roman feudalism were to be found in India, which ought therefore to be regarded as feudal, Marx points out that "Kovalevsky forgets among other things serfdom, which is not of substantial importance in India. (Moreover, as for the *individual role* of feudal lords as *protectors* not only of unfree but of free peasants . . . this is unimportant in India except for the *wakuf* (estates devoted to religious purposes).) Nor do we find that 'poetry of the soil' so characteristic of Romano-Germanic feudalism (cf. Maurer) in India, any more than in Rome. In India the land is nowhere *noble* in such a way as to be, e.g., inalienable to non-members of the noble class (roturiers)."[1] Engels, more interested in the possible combinations of lordship and the substratum of the primitive community, seems less categoric, though he specifically excludes the Orient from feudalism[2] and as we have seen, makes no attempt to extend his analysis of agrarian feudalism beyond Europe. There is nothing to suggest that Marx and Engels regarded the special combination of agrarian feudalism and the medieval city as anything except peculiar to Europe.

On the other hand a very interesting elaboration of the concept of social relations of production is sug-

[1] Quoted in L. S. Gamayunov, R. A. Ulyanovsky: "The Work of the Russian Sociologist M. M. Kovalevsky . . . and K. Marx's criticism of the work," *XXV International Congress of Orientalists*, Moscow, 1960, p. 8.

[2] *Anti-Dühring, loc. cit.,* 164.

gested by a number of passages in these later years. Here again it seems that Engels took the initiative. Thus of serfdom he writes (to Marx, 22.12.1882— possibly following a suggestion by Marx): "It is certain that serfdom and villeinage are not a specifically medieval-feudal form, it occurs everywhere or almost everywhere, where conquerors have made the native inhabitants cultivate the soil for them." And again, about wage-labour:[1] "The first capitalists already encountered wage-labour as a form. But they found it as something ancillary, exceptional or makeshift, or a point of passage." This distinction between modes of production characterised by certain relations, and the "forms" of such relations which can exist in a variety of periods or socio-economic settings, is already implicit in earlier Marxian thought. Sometimes, as in the discussion of money and mercantile activities, it is explicit. It has considerable importance, for not only does it help us dismiss such primitive arguments as those which deny the novelty of capitalism because merchants existed in ancient Egypt, or medieval manors paid their harvest-labour in money, but it draws attention to the fact that the basic social relations which are necessarily limited in number, are "invented" and "reinvented" by men on numerous occasions, and that all monetary modes of production (except perhaps capitalism) are complexes made up from all sorts of combinations of them.

V

Finally, it is worth surveying briefly the discussion on the main socio-economic formation among Marxists since the death of Marx and Engels. This has in many respects been unsatisfactory, though it has the advantage of never regarding Marx's and Engels' texts as embodying final truth. They have, in fact, been

[1] *Anti-Dühring*, loc. cit., 252.

extensively revised. However, the process of this revision has been strangely unsystematic and unplanned, the theoretical level of much of the discussion disappointing, and the subject has, on the whole, been confused rather than clarified.

Two tendencies may be noted. The first, which implies a considerable simplification of Marx's and Engels' thought, reduces the chief socio-economic formations to a single ladder which all human societies climb rung by rung, but at different speeds, so that all eventually arrive at the top.[1] This has some advantages from the point of view of politics and diplomacy, because it eliminates the distinction between societies which have shown a greater and those with a lesser built-in tendency to rapid historical development in the past, and because it makes it difficult for particular countries to claim that they are exceptions to general historical laws,[2] but it has no obvious scientific advantages, and is also at variance with Marx's views. Moreover, it is quite unnecessary politically, since, whatever the differences in past historical development, Marxism has always firmly held the view that all peoples, of whatever race or historical background, are equally capable of all the achievements of modern civilisation once they are free to pursue them.

The unilinear approach also leads to the search for "fundamental laws" of each formation, which explain their passing to the next-higher form. Such general mechanisms were already suggested by Marx and

[1] "All peoples travel what is basically the same path. . . . The development of society proceeds through the consecutive replacement, according to definite laws, of one socio-economic formation by another." O. Kuusinen ed. *Fundamentals of Marxism-Leninism* (London, 1961), 153.

[2] The fear of encouraging "Asiatic exceptionalism" and of discouraging a sufficiently firm opposition to (western) imperialist influence, was a strong, and perhaps the decisive, element in the abandonment of Marx's "Asiatic mode" by the international communist movement after 1930. Cf. the 1931 Leningrad discussions, as reported (very tendentiously) in K. A. Wittfogel, *Asiatic Despotism* (1957), 402-4. The Chinese Communist Party had independently taken the same road some years earlier. For its views, which appear to be very standard and unilinear, cf. Mao Tsetung, *Sel. Works*, III, 74-7.

Engels (notably in *Origin of the Family*) for the passage from the admittedly universal primitive communal stage to class society, and for the very different development of capitalism. A number of attempts have been made recently to discover analogous "general laws" of feudalism[1] and even of the slave-stage.[2] These have, by general consent, not been very successful, and even the formulae finally suggested for agreement seem to be little more than definitions. This failure to discover generally acceptable "fundamental laws" applicable to feudalism and slave-society is in itself not insignificant.

The second tendency partly follows from the first, but is also partly in conflict with it. It has led to a formal revision of Marx's list of socio-economic formations, by omitting the "Asiatic mode", limiting the scope of the "ancient", but correspondingly extending that of the "feudal". The omission of the "Asiatic mode" occurred, broadly speaking, between the late 1920s and the late 1930s: it is no longer mentioned in Stalin's *Dialectical and Historical Materialism* (1938), though it continued to be used by some—mainly English-speaking-Marxists—much later.[3] Since the characteristic for Marx was resistance to historical evolution, its elimination produces a simpler scheme which lends itself more readily to universal and unilinear interpretations. But it also eliminates the error of regarding oriental societies as essentially "unchanging" or a-historical. It has been remarked that "what Marx himself said about India cannot be taken as it stands", though also that "the theoretical basis (of the

[1] For the Soviet discussions of the early 1950s, cf. *Voprosi Istorii*, 6, 1953; 2, 1954; 2, 4 and 5, 1955. For the Western discussion on the transition from feudalism, which partly touches on similar themes, cf. *The Transition from Feudalism to Capitalism*, by P. M. Sweezy, M. H. Dobb, H. K. Takahashi, R. H. Hilton, C. Hill (London, n.d.). Also G. Lefebvre, *La Pensée*, 65, 1956; G. Procacci, *Società*, 1, 1955.

[2] Cf. Guenther & Schrot, *Problèmes théoriques de la société esclavagiste*, in *Recherches Internationales à la lumière du marxisme* (Paris) 2, May-June 1957.

[3] e.g. E. M. S. Namboodiripad, *The National Question in Kerala* (Bombay, 1952).

history of India) remains Marxist"[1]. The restriction of the "ancient" mode has posed no major political problems or (apparently) reflected political debates. It has been due simply to the failure of scholars to discover a slave-phase everywhere, and to find the rather simple model of the slave-economy which had become current (much simpler than Marx's own) adequate even for the classical societies of antiquity.[2] Official Soviet science is no longer committed to a universal stage of slave-society.[3]

"Feudalism" has expanded its scope partly to fill the gap left by these changes—none of the societies affected could be reclassified as capitalist or were reclassified as primitive-communal or "archaic" (as we remember that Marx and Engels inclined to do), and partly at the expense of societies hitherto classified as primitive communal, and of the earlier stages of capitalist development. For it is now clear that class differentiation in some societies formerly loosely called "tribal" (e.g. in many parts of Africa) had made considerable progress. At the other end of the time-scale the tendency to classify all societies as "feudal" until a formal "bourgeois revolution" had taken place, made some headway, notably in Britain.[4] But "feudalism" has not grown merely as a residual category. Since very early post-Marxist times there have been attempts to see a sort of primitive or proto-feudalism as the first general—though not necessarily universally occurring—form of class society growing out of the disintegration of primitive communalism.[5] (Such direct

[1] D. D. Kosambi, *An Introduction to the Study of Indian History* (Bombay, 1956), 11-12.
[2] Cf. *Recherches Internationales, loc. cit.* (1957), for a selection of studies.
[3] E. Zhukov, "The Periodization of World History", *International Historical Congress, Stockholm* 1960: *Rapports* I, 74-88, esp. 77.
[4] Cf. "State and Revolution in Tudor and Stuart England", *Communist Review*, July 1948. This view has, however, always had its critics, especially J. J. Kuczynski (*Geschichte d. Lage d. Arbeiter unter dem Kapitalismus*, vol. 22, cap. 1-2).
[5] Cf. Bogdanov, *Short Course of Economic Science*, 1897, revised 1919 (London, 1927), and, in a more sophisticated form, K. A. Wittfogel, *Geschichte der bürgerlichen Gesellschaft* (Vienna, 1924).

transition from primitive communalism to feudalism is of course provided for by Marx and Engels.) Out of this proto-feudalism, it is suggested, the various other formations developed, including the developed feudalism of the European (and Japanese) type. On the other hand a reversion to feudalism from formations which, while *potentially* less progressive, are in actual fact more highly developed—as from the Roman Empire to the tribal Teutonic kingdoms—has always been allowed for. Owen Lattimore goes so far as "to suggest that we think, experimentally, in terms of evolutionary and relapse (or devolutionary) feudalism", and also asks us to bear in mind the possibility of the temporary feudalisation of tribal societies interacting with more developed ones.[1]

The net result of all these various tendencies has been to bring into currency a vast category of "feudalism" which spans the continents and the millennia, and ranges from, say, the emirates of Northern Nigeria to France in 1788, from the tendencies visible in Aztec society on the eve of the Spanish conquest to Tsarist Russia in the nineteenth century. It is indeed likely that all these can be brought under one such general classification, and that this has analytical value. At the same time it is clear that without a good deal of sub-classification and the analysis of sub-types and individual historical phases, the general concept risks becoming much too unwieldy. Various such sub-classifications have been attempted, e.g. "semi-feudal", but so far the Marxist clarification of feudalism has not made adequate progress.

The combination of the two tendencies noted nere has produced one or two incidental difficulties. Thus the desire to classify every society or period firmly in one or another of the accepted pigeon-holes has produced demarcation disputes, as is natural when we

[1] O. Lattimore, "Feudalism in History", *Past and Present*, 12, 1957.

insist on fitting dynamic concepts into static ones. Thus there has been much discussion in China about the date of the transition from slavery to feudalism, since "the struggle was of a very protracted nature covering several centuries. . . . Different social and economic modes of life had temporarily coexisted on the vast territory of China."[1] In the West a similar difficulty has led to discussions about the character of the centuries from the fourteenth to the eighteenth.[2] These discussions have at least the merit of raising problems of the mixture and coexistence of different "forms" of social relations of production, though otherwise their interest is not as great as that of some other Marxist discussions.[3]

However, recently, and partly under the stimulus of the *Formen*, Marxist discussion has shown a welcome tendency to revive, and to question several of the views which have come to be accepted over the past few decades. This revival appears to have begun independently, in a number of countries, both socialist and non-socialist. A recent survey lists contributions from France, the German Democratic Republic, Hungary, Britain, India, Japan and Egypt.[4] These deal partly with general problems of historical periodisation, such as are discussed in the debate in *Marxism Today*, 1962, partly with the problems of specific pre-capitalist socio-economic formations, partly with the vexed and now re-opened question of the "Asiatic mode".[5] It is too early to do more than record the resumption of such discussions.

[1] E. Zhukov, *loc. cit.*, 78.
[2] *The Transition from Feudalism to Capitalism*, *loc. cit.*
[3] Cf. *Zur Periodisierung des Feudalismus und Kapitalismus in der Geschichtlichen Entwicklung der U.S.S.R.*, Berlin, 1952.
[4] *Asiaticus*, Il modo di produzione Asiatico (*Rinascita*, Rome, October 5, 1963, 14).
[5] *Recherches Internationales* 37 (May-June 1963), which deals with feudalism, contains some relevant polemical contributions. For ancient society, cf. the debates between Welskopf (*Die Produktionsverhältnisse im Alten Orient und in her griechisch-römischen Antike*, Berlin, 1957) and Guenther and Schrot (*Ztschr f. Geschichtswissenschaft*, 1957, and *Wissensch. Ztschr. d. Karl-Marx-Univ.*, Leipzig, 1963), for oriental society, F. Tökei, *Sur le mode de production asiatique*, Paris, Centre d'Etudes et de Recherches Marxistes, 1964, cyclostyled.

We may conclude that the present state of Marxist discussion in this field is unsatisfactory. Much of this is due to the historic developments in the international Marxist movement in the generation before the middle 1950s, which had an unquestionably negative effect on the level of Marxist discussion in this as in many other fields. Marx's original approach to the problem of historical evolution has been in some respects simplified and changed, and such reminders of the profound and complex nature of his methods as the publication of the *Formen*, have not been used to correct these tendencies. Marx's original list of socioeconomic formations has been altered, but no satisfactory substitute has yet been provided. Some of the gaps in Marx's and Engels' brilliant, but incomplete and tentative, discussion have been discovered and filled, but some of the most fruitful parts of their analysis have also been allowed to sink from sight.

This is all the more regrettable, because the past thirty years or so have been in many respects a period of great success for the Marxist approach to history. Indeed, one of the most convincing pieces of evidence for the superiority of the Marxist method is that even in a period when creative Marxism was only too often allowed to ossify, historical materialism nevertheless inspired a great deal of valuable historical work, and influenced non-Marxist historians more than ever before. All the more reason why today the much-needed clarification at the Marxist view of historical evolution, and especially the main stages of development, should be undertaken. A careful study of the *Formen*—which does not mean the automatic acceptance of all Marx's conclusions—can only help in this task, and is indeed an indispensable part of it.

E. J. HOBSBAWM

.

Pre-Capitalist Economic Formations

I

*ONE of the prerequisites of wage labour and one of the historic conditions for capital is free labour, and the exchange of free labour against money, in order to reproduce money and to convert it into values, in order to be consumed by money, not as use value for enjoyment, but as use value for money. Another prerequisite is the separation of free labour from the objective conditions of its realisation—from the means and material of labour. This means above all that the worker must be separated from the land, which functions as his natural laboratory. This means the dissolution both of free petty landownership and of communal landed property, based on the oriental commune.

In both these forms the relationship of the worker to the objective conditions of his labour is one of ownership: this is the natural unity of labour with its material prerequisites. Hence the worker has an objective existence independent of his labour. The individual is related to himself as a proprietor, as master of the conditions of his reality. The same relation holds between one individual and the rest. Where this *prerequisite* derives from the community, the others are his co-owners, who are so many incarnations of the common property. Where it derives from the individual families which jointly constitute the community, they are independent owners coexisting with him, independent private proprietors. The common property which formerly absorbed everything and embraced them all, then subsists as a special *ager publicus* (*common land*) separate from the numerous private owners.

* In both cases individuals behave not as labourers but as owners—and as members of a community who also labour. The purpose of this labour is not the *creation of value*, although they may perform surplus labour in order to exchange it for *foreign* labour, i.e. for surplus products. Its purpose is the maintenance of the owner and his family as well as of the communal body as a whole. The establishment of the individual as a *worker*, stripped of all qualities except this one, is itself a product of *history*.

* The first prerequisite of this earliest form of landed property appears as a human community, such as emerges from spontaneous evolution (*naturwüchsig*): the family, the family expanded into a tribe, or the tribe created by the inter-marriage of families or combination of tribes. We may take it for granted that pastoralism, or more generally a migratory life, is the first form of maintaining existence, the tribe not settling in a fixed place but using up what it finds locally and then passing on. Men are not settled by nature (unless perhaps in such fertile environments that they could subsist on a single tree like the monkeys; otherwise they would roam, like the wild animals). Hence the tribal community, the natural common body, appears not as the consequence, but as the precondition of the joint (temporary) appropriation and use of the soil.

Once men finally settle down, the way in which to a smaller degree this original community is modified, will depend on various external, climatic, geographical, physical, etc., conditions as well as on their special natural make-up—their tribal character. The spontaneously evolved tribal community, or, if you will, the herd—the common ties of blood, language, custom, etc.—is the first precondition of the appropriation of the objective conditions of life, and of the activity which reproduces and gives material expression to, or

objectifies (*vergegenständlichenden*) it (activity as herds-
men, hunters, agriculturalists, etc.). The earth is the
great laboratory, the arsenal which provides both the
means and the materials of labour, and also the location,
the *basis* of the community. Men's relation to it is
naïve: they regard themselves as its *communal proprietors*, and as those of the community which produces
and reproduces itself by living labour. Only in so far
as the individual is a member—in the literal and
figurative sense—of such a community, does he regard
himself as an owner or possessor. In reality *appropriation* by means of the process of labour takes place
under these *preconditions*, which are not the *product* of
labour but appear as its natural or *divine* preconditions.

Where the fundamental relationship is the same, this
form can realise itself in a variety of ways. For instance,
as is the case in most Asiatic fundamental forms it is
quite compatible with the fact that the *all-embracing
unity* which stands above all these small common bodies
may appear as the higher or *sole proprietor*, the real
communities only as *hereditary* possessors. Since the
unity is the real owner, and the real precondition of
common ownership, it is perfectly possible for it to
appear as something separate and superior to the
numerous real, particular communities. The individual
is then in fact propertyless, or property—i.e. the relationship of the individual to the *natural* conditions
of labour and reproduction, the inorganic nature
which he finds and makes his own, the objective body
of his subjectivity—appears to be mediated by means of
a grant (*Ablassen*) from the total unity to the individual
through the intermediary of the particular community.
The despot here appears as the father of all the numerous lesser communities, thus realising the common unity
of all. It therefore follows that the surplus product
(which, incidentally, is legally determined in terms of
[*infolge*] the real appropriation through labour) belongs

to this highest unity. Oriental despotism therefore appears to lead to a legal absence of property. In fact, however, its foundation is tribal or common property, in most cases created through a combination of manufacture and agriculture within the small community which thus becomes entirely self-sustaining and contains within itself all conditions of production and surplus production.

Part of its surplus labour belongs to the higher community, which ultimately appears as a *person*. This surplus labour is rendered both as tribute and as common labour for the glory of the unity, in part that of the despot, in part that of the imagined tribal entity of the god. In so far as this type of common property is actually realised in labour, it can appear in two ways. The small communities may vegetate independently side by side, and within each the individual labours independently with his family on the land allotted to him. (There will also be a certain amount of labour for the common store—for insurance as it were—on the one hand; and on the other for defraying the costs of the community as such, i.e. for war, religious worship, etc. The dominion of lords, in its most primitive sense, arises only at this point, e.g. in the Slavonic and Rumanian communities. Here lies the transition to serfdom, etc.) Secondly, the unity can involve a common organisation of labour itself, which in turn can constitute a veritable system, as in Mexico, and especially Peru, among the ancient Celts, and some tribes of India. Furthermore, the communality within the tribal body may tend to appear either as a representation of its unity through the head of the tribal kinship group, or as a relationship between the heads of families. Hence either a more despotic or a more democratic form of the community. The communal conditions for real appropriation through labour, such as irrigation systems (very important among the Asian peoples), means of communication, etc., will then appear as the work of the higher unity—the despotic government which is poised above the lesser communities. Cities in the proper sense arise by the side of these villages only where the location is particularly favourable to external trade, or where the head of the state and his satraps exchange their revenue (the surplus product) against labour, which they expend as labour-funds.

* The second form (of property) has, like the first, given rise to substantial variations, local, historical, etc. It is the product of a more dynamic (*bewegten*) historical life, of the fate and modification of the original tribes. The *community* is here also the first precondition, but unlike our first case, it is not here the substance of which the individuals are mere accidents (*Akzidenzen*) or of which they form mere spontaneously natural parts. The basis here is not the land, but the city as already created seat (centre) of the rural population (landowners). The cultivated area appears as the territory of the city; not, as in the other case, the village as a mere appendage to the land. However great the obstacles the land may put in the way of those who till it and really appropriate it, it is not difficult to establish a relationship with it as the inorganic nature of the living individual, as his workshop, his means of labour, the object of his labour and the means of subsistence of the subject. The difficulties encountered by the organised community can arise only from other communities which have either already occupied the land or disturb the community in its occupation of it. War is therefore the great all-embracing task, the great communal labour, and it is required either for the occupation of the objective conditions for living existence or for the protection and perpetuation of such occupation. The community, consisting of kinship groups, is therefore in the first instance organised on military lines, as a warlike, military force, and this is one of the conditions of its existence as a proprietor. Concentration of settlement in the city is the foundation of this warlike organisation. The nature of tribal structure leads to the differentiation of kinship groups into higher and lower, and this social differentiation is developed further by the mixing of conquering and conquered tribes, etc. Common land—as state property, *ager publicus*—is here separate from private property. The property of the individual, unlike our first case, is here not direct communal property, where the individual is not an owner in separation from the community, but rather its occupier. Circumstances arise in which individual property does not require communal labour for its valorisation (e.g. as it does in the irrigation systems of the Orient); the purely primitive character of the tribe may be broken by the movement of history or migration; the tribe may remove from its original place of settlement and occupy *foreign* soil, thus entering substantially new conditions of labour and developing the energies of the individual further. The more such factors operate— and the more the communal character of the tribe therefore appears, and must appear, rather as a negative unity as against the outside world—the more do conditions arise which allow the individual to become a *private proprietor* of land—of a particular plot—whose special cultivation belongs to him and his family.

The community—as a state—is, on the one hand, the relationship of these free and equal private proprietors to each other, their combination against the outside world—and at the same time their safeguard. The community is based on the fact that its members consist of working owners of land, small peasant cultivators; but in the same measure the independence of the latter consists in their mutual relation as members of the community, in the safeguarding of the *ager publicus* (common land) for common needs and common glory, etc. To be a member of the community remains the precondition for the appropriation of land, but in his capacity as member of the community the individual is a private proprietor. His relation to his private property is both a relation to the land and to his existence as a member of the community, and his maintenance as a member is the maintenance of the community, and vice versa, etc. Since the community, though it is here not merely a de facto *product of history*, but one of which men are conscious as such, has therefore *had an origin*, we have here the precondition for *property* in land—i.e. for the relation of the working subject to the natural conditions of his labour as belonging to him. But this "belonging" is mediated through his existence as a member of the state, through the existence of the state—hence through a *precondition* which is regarded as divine, etc.[1] There is concentration in the city, with the land as its territory; small-scale agriculture producing for immediate consumption; manufacture as the domestic subsidiary, labour of wives and daughters (spinning and weaving) or achieving independent existence in a few craft occupations (*fabri*, etc.). The precondition for the continued existence of the community is the maintenance of equality among its free self-sustaining peasants, and their individual labour as the condition of the continued existence of their property. Their relation to the natural conditions of labour are those of proprietors; but personal labour must continuously establish these conditions as real conditions and objective elements of the personality of the individual, of his personal labour.

On the other hand the tendency of this small warlike community drives it beyond these limits, etc. (Rome,

---

[1] An alternative translation would be: "Since the community . . . origin (and is thus) here the precondition . . . , this belonging is, however, mediated by . . ." Marx's habit of occasionally omitting auxiliary verbs makes it impossible always to interpret his meaning unambiguously.

Greece, Jews, etc.). As Niebuhr says: "When the auguries had assured Numa of the divine approval for his election, the first preoccupation of the pious monarch was not the worship of the gods, but a human one. He distributed the land conquered in war by Romulus and left to be occupied: he founded the worship of Terminus (the god of boundary-stones). All the ancient law-givers, and above all Moses founded the success of their arrangements for virtue, justice and good morals (*Sitte*) upon landed property, or at least on secure hereditary possession of land, for the greatest possible number of citizens" (Vol. I, 245, 2nd ed. *Roman History*). The individual is placed in such condition of gaining his life as to make not the acquiring of wealth his object, but self-sustenance, its own reproduction as a member of the community; the reproduction of himself as a proprietor of the parcel of ground and, in that quality, as a member of the commune.[1] The continuation of the commune is the reproduction of all its members as self-sustaining peasants, whose surplus time belongs precisely to the commune, the labour of war, etc. Ownership of one's labour is mediated through the ownership of the conditions of labour—the plot of land, which is itself guaranteed by the existence of the community, which in turn is safeguarded by the surplus labour of its members in the form of military service, etc. The member of the community reproduces himself not through co-operation in wealth-producing labour, but in co-operation in labour for the (real or imaginary) communal interests aimed at sustaining the union against external and internal stress (*nach aussen und innen*). Property formally belongs to the Roman citizen, the private owner of land is such only by virtue of being Roman, but any Roman is also a private landowner.

Another form of the property of working individuals,

---

[1] This sentence in English in the original.

self-sustaining members of the community, in the natural conditions of their labour, is the *Germanic*. Here the member of the community as such is not, as in the specifically oriental form, co-owner of the communal property. (Where property exists *only* as communal property, the individual member as such is only the *possessor* of a particular part of it, hereditary or not, for any fraction of property belongs to no member for himself, but only as the direct part of the community, consequently as someone in direct unity with the community and not as distinct from it. The individual is therefore only a possessor. What exists is only *communal* property and *private possession*. Historic and local, etc., circumstances may modify the character of this possession in its relation to the communal property in very different ways, depending on whether labour is performed in isolation by[1] the private possessor or is in turn determined by the community, or by the unity standing above the particular community.) Neither is the land [in the Germanic community—E.H.] occupied by the community as in the Roman, Greek (in brief, the ancient classical) form as Roman land. [In classical antiquity—E.H.] Part of it remains with the community as such, as distinct from the members, *ager publicus* (common land) in its various forms; the remainder is distributed, each plot of land being Roman by virtue of the fact that it is the private property, the domain, of a Roman, the share of the laboratory which is his; conversely he is Roman only, in so far as he possesses this sovereign right over part of the Roman soil.[2] [In antiquity urban crafts and trade were held in low, but agriculture in high, esteem; in the Middle Ages their status was reversed.] [The right of *use* of common

---

[1] *von*. This may be read either as "in isolation from" or "in isolation by". The second reading is preferred, making more sense in this context.
[2] The ensuing passages enclosed in square brackets, from "In antiquity urban crafts . . ." to "constitute a clan" are noted down by Marx from Niebuhr's *Roman History*; I, 418, 436, 614, 615, 317-19, 328-31, 333, 335.

land by *possession* originally belonged to the Patricians, who later granted it to their clients; the *assignment of property* out of the *ager publicus* belonged exclusively to the Plebeians; all assignments in favour of Plebeians and compensation for a share in the common land. *Landed property in the strict sense*, if we except the area surrounding the city wall, was originally in the hands only of the Plebeians (rural communities subsequently absorbed).] [Essence of the Roman Plebs as a totality of agriculturalists, as described in their quiritarian (citizen) property. The ancients unanimously commended farming as the *activity proper* to free men, the school for soldiers. The ancient stock[1] of the nation is preserved in it; it changes in the towns, where foreign merchants and artisans settle, as the natives migrate there, attracted by the hope of gain. Wherever there is slavery, the freedman seeks his subsistence in such activities, often accumulating wealth: hence in antiquity such occupations were generally in their hands and therefore unsuitable for citizens: hence the view that the admission of craftsmen to full citizenship was a hazardous procedure (the Greeks, as a rule, excluded them from it). "No Roman was permitted to lead the life of a petty trader or craftsman." The ancients had no conception of gild pride and dignity, as in medieval urban history; and even there the military spirit declined as the gilds vanquished the (aristocratic) lineages, and was finally extinguished; as, consequently also the respect in which the city was held outside and its freedom.]

[The tribes (*Stämme*) of the ancient states were constituted in one of two ways, either by *kinship* or by *locality*. *Kinship tribes* historically precede locality tribes, and are almost everywhere displaced by them. Their most extreme and rigid form is the institution of castes, separated from one another, without the right of inter-marriage, with quite different status; each with

---

1 The word *Stamm* can also be read as "tribe".

its exclusive, unchangeable occupation. The *locality* tribes originally corresponded to a division of the area into districts (*Gaue*) and villages; so that in Attica under Kleisthenes, any man settled in a village was registered as a Demotes (villager) of that village, and as a member of the Phyle (tribe) of the area to which that village belonged. However, as a rule his descendants, regardless of place of domicile, remained in the same Phyle and the same Deme, thereby giving to this division an appearance of ancestral descent. The Roman *kin-groups* (*gentes*) did not consist of blood-relatives; Cicero notes, when mentioning the family name, descent from free men. The members of the Roman gens had common shrines (*sacra*), but this had already disappeared in Cicero's day. The joint inheritance from fellow-kinsmen who died intestate or without close relatives, was retained longest of all. In most ancient times, members of the *gens* had the obligation to assist fellow-kinsmen in need of assistance to bear unusual burdens. (This occurs universally among the Germans, and persisted longest among the Dithmarschen.) The *gentes* a sort of gild. A more general organisation than that of kin groups did not exist in the ancient world. Thus among the Gaels, the aristocratic Campbells and their vassals constitute a clan.] Since the Patrician represents the community to a higher degree, he is the *possessor* of the *ager publicus*, and uses it through the intermediary of his clients, etc. (also, gradually appropriates it).

The Germanic community is not concentrated in the city; a concentration—the city the centre of rural life, the domicile of the land workers, as also the centre of warfare—which gives the community as such an external existence, distinct from that of its individual members. Ancient classical history is the history of cities, but cities based on landownership and agriculture; Asian history is a kind of undifferentiated unity of town and country (the large city, properly speaking, must be regarded merely as a princely camp, superimposed on the real economic structure); the Middle Ages (Germanic period) starts with the countryside as the locus of history, whose further development then proceeds through the opposition of town and country; modern (history) is the urbanisation of the countryside, not, as among the ancients, the ruralisation of the city.

* ¹Union in the city gives the community as such an economic existence; the mere *presence* of the town as such is different from a mere mutiplicity of separate houses. Here the whole does not consist of its separate parts. It is a form of independent organism. Among the Germans, where single heads of families settle in the forests, separated by long distances, even on an *external* view the community exists merely by virtue of every act of union of its members, although their unity *existing in itself* is embodied (*gesetzt*) in descent, language, common past and history, etc. The *community* therefore appears as an *association*, not as a *union*, as an agreement (*Einigung*), whose independent subjects are the landowners, and not as a unity. In fact, therefore, the community has no existence as a *state*, a *political entity* as among the ancients, because it has no existence as a *city*. If the community is to enter upon real existence, the free landowners must hold an *assembly*, whereas, e.g., in Rome it *exists* apart from such assemblies, in the presence of the *city itself* and the officials placed at its head, etc.

True, the *ager publicus*, the common land or peoples' land, occurs among the Germans also, as distinct from the property of individuals. It consists of hunting grounds, common pastures or woodlands, etc., as that part of the land which cannot be partitioned if it is to

---

¹ Here begins a new notebook of Marx's manuscript, entitled "Notebook V. Chapter on capital. Continued". It is dated January 1858 (begun January 22.)

serve as a means of production in this specific form. However, unlike the Roman case, the *ager publicus* does not appear as the particular economic being of the state, by the side of the private owners—who are properly speaking private proprietors as such in so far as they have been *excluded* from or deprived of the use of the *ager publicus*, like the Plebeians. The *ager publicus* appears rather as a mere supplement to individual property among the Germans, and figures as property only in so far as it is defended against hostile tribes as the common property of one tribe. The property of the individual does not appear mediated through the community, but the existence of the community and of communal property as mediated through—i.e. as a mutual relation of—the independent subjects.

At bottom every individual household contains an entire economy, forming as it does an independent centre of production (manufacture merely the domestic subsidiary labour of the women, etc.). In classical antiquity the city with its attached territory formed the economic whole, in the Germanic world, the individual home, which itself appears merely as a point in the land belonging to it; there is no concentration of a multiplicity of proprietors, but the family as an independent unit. In the Asiatic form (or at least predominantly so) there is no property, but only individual possession; the community is properly speaking the real proprietor, —hence property only as *communal property* in land. In antiquity (Romans as the classic example, the thing in its purest and most clearly marked form), there is a contradictory form of state landed property and private landed property, so that the latter is mediated through the former, or the former exists only in this double form. The private landed proprietor is therefore simultaneously an urban citizen. Economically citizenship may be expressed more simply as a form in which the agriculturalist lives in a city. In the Germanic form the agriculturalist is not a citizen, i.e. not an inhabitant of cities, but its foundation is the isolated, independent family settlement, guaranteed by means of its association with other such settlements by men of the same tribe, and their occasional assembly for purposes of war, religion, the settlement of legal disputes, etc., which establishes their mutual surety. Individual landed property does not here appear as a contradictory form of communal landed property, nor as mediated by the community, but the other way round. The community exists only in the mutual relation of the individual landowners as such. Communal property as such appears only as a communal accessory to the individual kin settlements and land appropriations. The community is neither the substance, of which the individual appears merely as the accident, nor is it the general, which *exists and has being* as such in men's minds, and in the reality of the city and its urban requirements, distinct from the separate economic being of its members. It is rather on the one hand, the common element in language, blood, etc., which is the premise of the individual proprietor; but on the other hand it has real being only in its *actual assembly* for communal purposes; and, in so far as it has a separate economic existence, in the communally used hunting-grounds, pastures, etc., it is used thus by every individual proprietor as such, and not in his capacity as the representative of the state (as in Rome). It is genuinely the common property of the individual owners, and not of the union of owners, possessing an existence of its own in the city, distinct from that of the individual members.

* The crucial point here is this: in all these forms, where landed property and agriculture form the basis of the economic order and consequently the economic object is the production of use values, i.e. the *reproduc-*

tion of the individual in certain definite relationships to his community, of which it forms the basis, we find the following elements:

1. Appropriation of the natural conditions of labour, of the *earth* as the original instrument of labour, both laboratory and repository of its raw materials; however, appropriation not by means of labour, but as the preliminary condition of labour. The individual simply regards the objective conditions of labour as his own, as the inorganic nature of his subjectivity, which realises itself through them. The chief objective condition of labour itself appears not as the *product* of labour, but occurs as *nature*. On the one hand we have the living individual, on the other the earth, as the objective condition of his reproduction.

2. The *attitude* to the land, to the earth as the property of the working individual, means that a man appears from the start as something more than the abstraction of the "working individual", but has an *objective mode of existence* in his ownership of the earth, which is *antecedent* to his activity and does not appear as its mere consequence, and is as much a precondition of his activity as his skin, his senses, for whole skin and sense organs are also developed, reproduced, etc., in the process of life, they are also presupposed by it. What immediately mediates this attitude is the more or less naturally evolved, more or less historically evolved and modified existence of the individual as *a member of a community*—his primitive existence as part of a tribe, etc.

An isolated individual could no more possess property in land than he could speak. At most he could live off it as a source of supply, like the animals. The relation to the soil as property always arises through the peaceful or violent occupation of the land by the tribe or the community in some more or less primitive or already historically developed form. The individual here can never appear in the total isolation of the mere free labourer. If the objective conditions of his labour are presumed to belong to him, he himself is subjectively presumed to belong to a community which mediates his relationship to the objective conditions of labour. Conversely, the real existence of the community is determined by the specific form of its ownership of the objective conditions of labour. The property mediated by its existence in a community, may appear as *communal property*, which gives the individual only possession and no private property in the soil; or else it may appear in the dual form of state and private property which coexist side by side, but in such a way as to make the former the precondition of the latter, so that only the citizen is and must be a private proprietor, while on the other hand his property *qua* citizen also has a separate existence. Lastly, communal property may appear merely as a supplement to private property, which in this case forms the basis; in this case the community has no existence except in the *assembly* of its members and in their association for common purposes.

These different forms of relationship of communal tribal members to the tribal land—to the earth upon which it has settled—depend partly on the natural character (*Naturanlagen*) of the tribe, partly on the economic conditions in which the tribe really exercises its ownership of the land, i.e. appropriates its fruits by means of labour. And this in turn will depend on the climate, the physical properties of the soil, the physically conditioned mode of its utilisation, the relationships to hostile or neighbouring tribes, and such modifications as are introduced by migrations, historical events, etc. If the community as such is to continue in the old way, the reproduction of its members under the objective conditions already assumed as given, is necessary. Production itself, the advance of population (which also falls under the head of production), in time necessarily eliminates these conditions, destroying instead of reproducing them, etc., and as this occurs the community decays and dies, together with the property relations on which it was based.

The Asiatic form necessarily survives longest and most stubbornly. This is due to the fundamental principle on which it is based, that is, that the individual does not become independent of the community; that the circle of production is self-sustaining, unity of agriculture and craft manufacture, etc. If the individual changes his relation to the community, he modifies and undermines both the community and its economic premise; conversely, the modification of this economic premise—produced by its own dialectic, pauperisation, etc. Note especially the influence of warfare and conquest. While, e.g., in Rome this is an essential part of the economic conditions of the community itself, it breaks the real bond on which the community rests.

In all these forms the basis of evolution is the *reproduction* of relations between individual and community *assumed as given*—they may be more or less primitive, more or less the result of history, but fixed into tradition—and a *definite, predetermined objective* existence, both as regards the relation to the conditions of labour and the relation between one man and his co-workers, fellow-tribesmen, etc. Such evolution is therefore from the outset *limited*, but once the limits are transcended, decay and disintegration ensue. Evolution of slavery, concentration of landed property, exchange, a monetary economy, conquest, etc., as among the Romans. All these appeared nevertheless up to a point to be compatible with the base, and merely innocent extensions of it, or else mere abuses arising from it. Considerable developments are thus possible within a given sphere. Individuals may appear to be great. But free and full development of individual or society is inconceivable here, for such evolution stands in contradiction to the original relationship.

* Among the ancients we discover no single enquiry as to which form of landed property, etc., is the most productive, which creates maximum wealth. Wealth does not appear as the aim of production, although Cato may well investigate the most profitable cultivation of fields, or Brutus may even lend money at the most favourable rate of interest. The enquiry is always about what kind of property creates the best citizens. Wealth as an end in itself appears only among a few trading peoples—monopolists of the carrying trade— who live in the pores of the ancient world like the Jews in medieval society. Wealth is on the one hand a thing, realised in things, in material products as against man as a subject. On the other hand, in its capacity as value, it is the mere right to command other people's labour, not for the purpose of dominion, but of private enjoyment, etc. In all its forms it appears in the form of objects, whether of things or of relationships by means of things, which lie outside of, and as it were accidentally beside, the individual.

Thus the ancient conception, in which man always appears (in however narrowly national, religious or political a definition) as the aim of production, seems very much more exalted than the modern world, in which production is the aim of man and wealth the aim of production. In fact, however, when the narrow bourgeois form has been peeled away, what is wealth, if not the universality of needs, capacities, enjoyments, productive powers, etc., of individuals, produced in universal exchange? What, if not the full development of human control over the forces of nature—those of his own nature as well as those of so-called "nature"? What, if not the absolute elaboration of his creative dispositions, without any preconditions other than antecedent historical evolution which makes the totality of this evolution—i.e. the evolution of all human powers as such, unmeasured by any *previously established* yardstick—an end in itself? What is this, if not a situation where man does not reproduce himself in any determined form, but produces his totality? Where he does not seek to remain something formed by the past, but is in the absolute movement of becoming? In bourgeois political economy—and in the epoch of production to which it corresponds—this complete elaboration of what lies within man, appears as the total alienation, and the destruction of all fixed, one-sided purposes as the sacrifice of the end in itself to a wholly external compulsion. Hence in one way the childlike world of the ancients appears to be superior; and this is so, in so far as we seek for closed shape, form and established limitation. The ancients provide a narrow satisfaction, whereas the modern world leaves us unsatisfied, or, where it appears to be satisfied with itself, is *vulgar* and *mean*.[1]

  * What Mr. Proudhon calls the *extra-economic* origin of property—by which he means landed property—is the *pre-bourgeois* relationship of the individual to the objective conditions of labour, and in the first instance to the *natural* objective conditions of labour. For, just as the working subject is a natural individual, a natural being, so the first objective condition of his labour appears as nature, earth, as an inorganic body. He himself is not only the organic body, but also inorganic nature as a subject. This condition is not something he has produced, but something he finds to hand; something existing in nature and which he presupposes. Before proceeding in our analysis, a further point: poor Proudhon not only could, but ought equally to be

---

[1] The German *gemein* has a variety of (in this instance obviously pejorative) senses which cannot be reproduced in any single English word today.

obliged, to accuse *capital* and *wage-labour*—as forms of property—of *extra-economic* origin. For the fact that the worker finds the objective conditions of his labour as something separate from him, as *capital*, and the fact that the capitalist finds the *workers* propertyless, as abstract labourers—the exchange as it takes place between value and living labour—assumes a *historic process*, however much capital and wage-labour themselves reproduce this relationship and elaborate it in objective scope, as well as in depth. And this historic process, as we have seen, is the evolutionary history of both capital and wage-labour. In other words, the *extra-economic origin* of property merely means the historic origin of the bourgeois economy, of the forms of production to which the categories of political economy give theoretical or ideal expression. But to claim that pre-bourgeois history and each phase of it, has its own *economy*[1] and an *economic base* of its movement, is at bottom merely to state the tautology that human life has always rested on some kind of production—*social* production—whose relations are precisely what we call economic relations.

   * *The original conditions of production cannot* initially be *themselves produced*—they are not the results of production. (Instead of original conditions of production we might also say: for if this reproduction appears on one hand as the appropriation of the objects by the subjects, it equally appears on the other as the moulding, the subjection, of the objects by and to a subjective purpose; the transformation of the objects into results and repositories of subjective activity.) What requires explanation is not the *unity* of living and active human beings with the natural, inorganic conditions of their metabolism with nature, and therefore their appropriation of nature; nor is this the result

----

[1] Marx uses the word *Ökonomie* in this paragraph. It is not clear whether this should mean "economics" or "economy".

of a historic process. What we must explain is the *separation* of these inorganic conditions of human existence from this active existence, a separation which is only fully completed in the relationship between wage-labour and capital.

In the relationship of slavery and serfdom there is no such separation; what happens is that one part of society is treated by another as the mere *inorganic and natural* condition of its own reproduction. The slave stands in no sort of relation to the objective conditions of his labour. It is rather *labour* itself, both in the form of the slave as of the serf, which is placed among the other living things (*Naturwesen*) *as inorganic condition* of production, alongside the cattle or as an appendage of the soil. In other words: the original conditions of production appear as natural prerequisites, *natural conditions of existence of the producer*, just as his living body, however reproduced and developed by him, is not originally established by himself, but appears as his *prerequisite*; his own (physical) being is a natural prerequisite, not established by himself. These *natural conditions of existence*, to which he is related as to an inorganic body, have a dual character: they are (1) subjective and (2) objective. The producer occurs as part of a family, a tribe, a grouping of his people, etc.—which acquires historically differing shapes as the result of mixture and conflict with others. It is as such a communal part that he has his relation to a determined (piece of) nature (let us still call it earth, land, soil), as his own inorganic being, the condition of his production and reproduction. As the natural part of the community he participates in the communal property and takes a separate share into his own possession; just so, as a Roman citizen by birth, he has (at least) ideally a claim to the *ager publicus* and a real claim to so and so many *juggera* (units) of land, etc. His *property*, i.e. his relation to the natural prerequisites of his production as *his own*, is mediated by his natural membership of a community. (The abstraction of a community whose members have nothing in common but language, etc., and barely even that, is plainly the product of much later historical circumstances.) It is, for instance, evident that the individual is related to his language as *his own* only as the natural member of a human community. Language as the product of an individual is an absurdity. But so also is property.

* Language itself is just as much the product of a community, as in another respect it is the existence of the community: it is, as it were, the communal being speaking for itself. Communal production and communal ownership, as found, e.g., in Peru, is evidently a *secondary* form introduced and transmitted by conquering tribes, who amongst themselves[1] had been familiar with common ownership and communal production in the older and simpler form, such as occurs in India and among the Slavs. Similarly, the form found, e.g., among the Celts in Wales appears to have been introduced there by more advanced conquerors, and thus to be *secondary*. The completeness and systematic elaboration of these systems under (the direction of) a supreme authority demonstrate their later origins. Just so the feudalism introduced into England was formally more complete than the feudalism which had naturally grown up in France.

Among nomadic pastoral tribes—and all pastoral peoples are originally migratory—the earth, like all other conditions of nature, appears in its elementary boundlessness, e.g. in the Asian steppes and the Asian high plateaux. It is grazed, etc., consumed by the herds, which provide the nomadic peoples with their subsistence. They regard it as their property, though never fixing that property. This is the case with the hunting grounds of the wild Indian tribes of America: the tribe

[1] *bei sich selbst* may also mean: in their original habitat.

considers a certain region as its hunting territory and maintains it by force against other tribes, or seeks to expel other tribes from the territory they claim. Among the nomadic pastoral tribes the community is in fact always united, a travelling party, caravan, horde, and the forms of higher and lower rank develop out of the conditions of this mode of life. What is *appropriated* and *reproduced* is here only the herd and not the soil, which is always used in temporary commonalty wherever the tribe breaks its wanderings.

Let us pass on to the consideration of settled peoples. The only barrier which the community can encounter in its relations to the natural conditions of production *as its own*—to the land—is some *other community*, which has already laid claim to them as its inorganic body. War is therefore one of the earliest tasks of every primitive community of this kind, both for the defence of property and for its acquisition. (It will be sufficient to speak of original property in land, for among pastoral peoples property in such natural products of the earth as, e.g., sheep is at the same time property in the pastures they pass through. In general, property in land includes property in its organic products.) Where man himself is captured as an organic accessory of the land and together with it, he is captured as one of the conditions of production, and this is the origin of slavery and serfdom, which soon debase and modify the original forms of all communities, and themselves become their foundation. As a result the simple structure is thereby determined negatively.

* Thus originally *property* means no more than man's attitude to his natural conditions of production as belonging to him, as the *prerequisites of his own existence*; his attitude to them as *natural prerequisites* of himself, which constitute, as it were, a prolongation of his body. In fact he stands in no relation to his conditions of production, but has a double existence, subjectively as himself and objectively in these natural inorganic conditions of his being. The forms of these *natural conditions of production* have a double character: (1) his existence as part of a community, which in its original form is a tribal community, more or less modified; (2) his relation to the *land* as to *his own*,[1] in virtue of the community, communal landed property, at the same time *individual possession* for the individual, or in such a manner that the soil and its cultivation remain in common and only its products are divided. (However, *dwellings*, etc., even if no more than the waggons of the Scythians, nevertheless appear to be always in the possession of individuals.) Membership of a *naturally evolved society*, a tribe, etc., is a natural condition of production for the living individual. Such membership is, e.g., already a condition of his language, etc. His own productive existence is only possible under this condition. His subjective existence as such is conditioned by it as much as it is conditioned by the relationship to the earth as to his laboratory. (True, property is originally *mobile*, for in the first instance man takes possession of the ready-made fruits of the earth, including animals and especially those capable of domestication. However, even this situation—hunting, fishing, pastoralism, subsistence by collecting the fruit of the trees, etc.—always assumes the appropriation of the earth, whether as a place of fixed settlement or a territory for roaming, a pasture for his animals, etc.)

    * *Property* therefore means *belonging to a tribe* (community) (to have one's subjective/objective existence within it), and by means of the relationship of this community to the land, to the earth as its inorganic body, there occurs the relationship of the individual to the land, to the external primary condition of production—for the earth is at the same time raw material,

---

[1] *als dem seinigen* might also mean: as its (the community's) own,

tool and fruit—as the preconditions belonging to his individuality, as its modes of existence. We *reduce this property to the relationship to the conditions of production.* Why not to those of consumption, since originally the act of producing by the individual is confined to the reproduction of his own body through the appropriation of ready-made objects prepared by nature for consumption? But even where these have merely to be *found* and *discovered,* effort, labour—as in hunting, fishing, the care of flocks—and the production (i.e. the development) of certain capacities by the subject, are soon required. Moreover, conditions in which man need merely reach for what is already available, without any tools (i.e. without products of labour already designed for production), etc., are very transitory, and can nowhere be regarded as normal; not even as normal in the most primitive state. In addition, the original conditions of production automatically include matter directly consumable without labour, such as fruit, animals, etc.; consequently, the fund of consumption itself appears as a part of the *original fund of production.*

  * The fundamental condition of property based on tribalism (which is originally formed out of the community[1]) is to be a member of the tribe. Consequently a tribe conquered and subjugated by another becomes *propertyless* and part of the *inorganic conditions* of the conquering tribe's reproduction, which that community regards as its own. Slavery and serfdom are therefore simply further developments of property based on tribalism. They necessarily modify all its forms. This they are least able to do in the Asiatic form. In the self-sustaining unity of manufactures and agriculture on which this form is based, conquest is not so essential a condition as where *landed property, agriculture,* predominate exclusively. On the other hand, since the individual

---

[1] This obscure phrase reads in German: *auf dem Stammwesen (worein sich das Gemeinwesen ursprünglich auflöst.*

in this form never becomes an owner but only a possessor, he is at bottom himself the property, the slave of that which embodies the unity of the community. Here slavery neither puts an end to the conditions of labour, nor does it modify the essential relationship.

* It is therefore now evident that:

* In so far as property is merely a conscious attitude to the conditions of production as to *one's own*—an attitude established by the community for the individual, proclaimed and guaranteed as law; in so far as the existence of the producer therefore appears as an existence within the objective conditions *belonging to him*, it is realised only through production. Actual appropriation takes place not through the relationship to these conditions as expressed in thought, but through the active, real relationship to them; in the process of positing them as the conditions of man's subjective activity.

* But this also clearly means that *these conditions change*. What makes a region of the earth into a hunting-ground, is being hunted over by tribes; what turns the soil into a prolongation of the body of the individual is agriculture. Once the *city of Rome* had been built and its surrounding land cultivated by its citizens, the conditions of the community were different from what they had been before. The object of all these communities is preservation, *i.e. the production of the individuals which constitute them as proprietors, i.e. in the same objective mode of existence, which also forms the relationship of the members to each other, and therefore forms the community itself. But this reproduction is at the same time necessarily new production and the destruction of the old form.*

For instance, where each individual is supposed to possess so many acres of land, the mere increase in population constitutes an obstacle. If this is to be overcome, colonisation will develop and this necessitates wars of conquest. This leads to slavery, etc., also, e.g., the enlargement of the *ager publicus*, and hence to the rise of the Patricians, who represent the community, etc.[1] Thus the preservation of the ancient community implies the destruction of the conditions upon which it rests, and turns into its opposite. Suppose, for instance, that productivity could be increased without increase in territory, by means of a development of the forces of production (which in agriculture, a most traditional occupation, are the slowest of all). This would imply new methods and combinations of labour, the high proportion of the day which would then have to be devoted to agriculture, etc., and once again the old economic conditions of the community would cease to operate. The act of reproduction itself changes not only the objective conditions—e.g. transforming village into town, the wilderness into agricultural clearings, etc.—but the producers change with it, by the emergence of new qualities, by transforming and developing themselves in production, forming new powers and new conceptions, new modes of intercourse, new needs, and new speech.

The more traditional the mode of production itself, i.e. the more the *real process* of appropriation remains the same, the more unchanging will the ancient forms of property be and therefore also the community as a whole. (Note that the traditional mode persists for a long time in agriculture and even longer in the oriental combination of agriculture and manufacture.) Where the members of the community have already acquired separate existence as private proprietors from their collective existence as an urban community and owners of the urban territory, conditions already arise which allow the individual to *lose* his property, i.e. the double relationship which makes him both a citizen with equal

[1] Marx's highly condensed phrase is not entirely unambiguous: *Damit Sklaven, etc. Vergrösserung des ager publicus z.B. auch, und damit die Patrizier, die das Gemeinwesen repräsentieren, etc.*

status, a member of the community, and a *proprietor*. In the oriental form this *loss* is hardly possible, except as a result of entirely external influences, for the individual member of the community never establishes so independent a relation to it as to enable him to lose his (objective, economic) tie with it. He is firmly rooted. This is also an aspect of the union of manufacture and agriculture, of town (in this instance the village) and country. Among the ancients manufacture already appears as corruption (fit business for freedmen, clients and foreigners), etc. Productive labour is freed from its pure subordination to agriculture, where it is the domestic labour of free persons, destined only for the purpose of farming, and war or religious observance and communal tasks such as the construction of houses, roads or temples. This development, which necessarily arises from intercourse with foreigners, from slaves, the desire to exchange the surplus product, etc., dissolves the mode of production upon which the community rests, and with it the *objectively individual man*—i.e. the individual determined as a Greek, a Roman, etc. Exchange has the same effect, and so has indebtedness, etc.

* We have an original unity between a specific form of community or tribal unit and the property in nature connected with it, or the relation to the objective conditions of production as naturally existing, as the objective being of the individual by means of the community. Now this unity, which in one sense appears as the particular form of property, has its living reality in a specific *mode of production* itself, and this mode appears equally as the relationship of the individuals to one another and as their specific daily behaviour towards inorganic nature, their specific mode of labour (which is always family labour and often communal labour). The community itself appears as the first great force of production; special kinds of conditions of

production (e.g. animal husbandry, agriculture) lead to the evolution of a special mode of production and special forces of production, both objective and subjective, the latter appearing as qualities of the individuals.

* In the last instance the community and the property resting upon it can be reduced to a specific stage in the development of the forces of production of the labouring subjects—to which correspond specific relations of these subjects with each other and with nature. Up to a certain point, reproduction. Thereafter, it turns into dissolution.

* *Property*—and this applies to its Asiatic, Slavonic ancient classical and Germanic forms—therefore originally signifies a relation of the working (producing) subject (or a subject reproducing himself) to the conditions of his production or reproduction as his own. Hence, according to the conditions of production, property will take different forms. The object of production itself is to reproduce the producer in and together with these objective conditions of his existence. This behaviour as a proprietor—which is not the result but the precondition of labour, i.e. of production—assumes a specific existence of the individual as part of a tribal or communal entity (whose property he is himself up to a certain point). Slavery, serfdom, etc., where the labourer himself appears among the natural conditions of production for a third individual or community—and where property therefore is no longer the relationship of the independently labouring individual to the objective conditions of labour—is always secondary, never primary, although it is the necessary and logical result of property founded upon the community and upon labour in the community. (This character of slavery does *not* apply to the general slavery of the orient, which is so considered *only* from the European point of view.)

It is of course easy to imagine a powerful, physically superior person, who first captures animals and then captures men in order to make them catch animals for him; in brief, one who uses man as a naturally occurring condition for his reproduction like any other living natural thing; his own labour being exhausted in the act of domination. But such a view is stupid, though it may be correct from the point of view of a given tribal or communal entity; for it takes the *isolated* man as its starting-point. But man is only individualised through the process of history. He originally appears as a *generic being, a tribal being, a herd animal*—though by no means as a "political animal" in the political sense. Exchange itself is a major agent of this individualisation. It makes the herd animal superfluous and dissolves it. Once the situation is such, that man as an isolated person has relation only to himself, the means of establishing himself as an isolated individual have become what gives him his general communal character.[1] In such a community the objective existence of the individual as a proprietor, say a landed proprietor, is presupposed, though he is a proprietor under certain conditions which chain him to the community, or rather constitute a link in his chain. In bourgeois society, e.g., the worker exists purely subjectively, without object; but the thing which *confronts* him has now become the *true common entity* which he seeks to devour and which devours him.

* All the forms in which the community imputes to the subjects a specific objective unity with the conditions of their production, or in which a specific subjective existence imputes the community itself as condition of production, necessarily correspond only to a development of the forces of production which is limited both in fact and in principle. (These forms are of course more or less naturally evolved, but at the

---

[1] *sein Sich-Allgemein-und-Gemeinmachen.*

same time also the results of a historic process.)The evolution of the forces of production dissolves them, and their dissolution is itself an evolution of the human forces of production. Labour is initially undertaken on a certain basis—first primitive—then historical.[1] Later, however, this basis or presupposition is itself cancelled, or tends to disappear, having become too narrow for the development of the progressive human horde.

* In so far as the landed property of classical antiquity reappears in modern allotment property, it belongs to political economy and we shall deal with it in the section on landed property.

* (All this is to be analysed again more deeply and in greater detail later.)

* What we are concerned with here is this: the relationship of labour to capital or to the objective conditions of labour as capital, presupposes a historic process which dissolves the different forms, in which the labourer is an owner and the owner labours. This means first and foremost:

(1) a *dissolution* of the relation to the earth—to land or soil—as a natural condition of production which man treats as his own inorganic being, the laboratory of his forces and the domain of his will. All forms in which this property is found, assume a *communal entity* whose members, whatever the formal distinctions between them, are *proprietors* by virtue of being its members. Hence the original form of this property is *direct communal property* (the *oriental form*, modified among the Slavs; developed to the point of contradiction in classical antiquity and Germanic property, though still the hidden, if antagonistic, foundation).

(2) *Dissolution of the relations* in which man appears as the *proprietor of the instrument.* As the above form of landed property assumes a *real community,* so this

---

[1] *Es wird erst gearbeitet von gewisser Grundlage aus—erst naturwüchsig—dann historische Voraussetzung.* The sentence is elliptic and open to various possible interpretations.

ownership of the tool by the labourer assumes a particular form of development of manufacture— namely, in the form of *handicraft labour*. Gild and corporative institutions are bound up with this. (The manufacturing activities of the ancient orient may be included under our heading (1) above.) Here labour itself is still half the expression of artistic creation, half its own reward, etc.[1] The institution of the "master craftsman". The capitalist himself still a master craftsman. Special craft skill itself ensures the ownership of the instrument, etc., etc. In a sense, the mode of labour becomes hereditary together with the organisation of labour and its instrument. Medieval town life. Labour still belongs to a man; a certain self-sufficient development of specialised (*einseitige*) capacities, etc.

(3) Included in both is the fact that man possesses means of consumption prior to production, necessary in order to enable him to keep alive as producer—i.e. in the course of production, *before* its completion. As a land-owner, he appears to be directly provided with the necessary fund for consumption. As a master artisan he had inherited, earned or saved this fund, and as a youngster he is still an *apprentice*, he does not yet appear as an independent worker in the strict sense, but shares the master's food in the patriarchal manner. As a (genuine) journeyman there is a certain common utilisation of the fund of consumption which is in the master's possession. Though this is not the journey-man's *property*, the laws and customs, etc., of the gild at least make him into a co-possessor. (This point to be elaborated.)

(4) On the other hand *dissolution* both of the relations under which the *labourers themselves*, the *living units of labour power* are still a *direct part of the objective conditions of production* and are appropriated as such—and

---

[1] *Hier die Arbeit selbst noch halb künstlerisch, halb Selbstzweck.*

are therefore slaves or serfs. For capital the worker does not constitute a condition of production, but only labour. If this can be performed by machinery, or even by water or air, so much the better. And what capital appropriates is not the labourer, but his labour—and not directly, but by means of exchange.

* These, then, on the one hand, are historic prerequisites without which the labourer cannot occur as free labourer, as objectiveless, purely subjective capacity for labouring, confronting the objective conditions of production as his *non-property*, as *someone else's property*, as *value* existing for itself, as capital. On the other hand, we must now ask what conditions are necessary if he is to confront *capital*.

II

* The formula "capital", in which living labour stands in the relation of non-property to raw material, instrument and the means of subsistence required during the period of production, implies in the first instance *non-property in land*; i.e. the absence of a state in which the working individual regards the land, the soil, as his own and labours as its proprietor. In the most favourable case he stands both in the relation of labourer to the land, and in the relation of landowner to himself in his capacity as a labouring subject. Potentially the ownership of land includes both property in raw materials, and in the original instrument of labour, the soil, as well as in its spontaneous fruits. In the most original form, this means that the individual regards the soil as belonging to him, and finds in it raw material, instrument, and means of subsistence not created by labour but by the earth itself. Once this relationship is reproduced, then secondary instruments and fruits of the earth produced by labour immediately appear included in the primitive form of landownership. It is this historic situation which is in the first instance negated by the more complete property-relationship involved in the relation of the worker to the conditions of labour as capital. This is historic situation No. 1 which is negated in the new relationship, or assumed to have been dissolved by history. A second historical step is implied in *property in the instrument*, i.e. in the relation of the labourer to the instruments as to his own, in which he labours as the owner of the instrument (which assumes that the instrument is subsumed in his individual labour, i.e. which assumes a special and limited phase of development of the productive force of labour). We are considering a situation in which the labourer not only owns the instrument, but in which this form of the *labourer as proprietor* or of the *labouring proprietor* is already distinct and separate from *landed property*, and not, as in the first case, an accident of landed property and subsumed under it: in other words, the artisan and urban development of labour. Hence, also, we here find raw material and means of subsistence *mediated* as the property of the artisan, mediated through his craft, through his property in the instrument. This second historic step now exists distinct and separate from the first, which in turn will appear considerably modified by the mere fact that *this second type of property* or of *working proprietor* has established its independent existence.

Since the instrument itself is already the product of labour, i.e. the element which constitutes property is already established by labour, the community can here no longer appear, as it can in the first case, in its primitive form. The community on which this form of property is based already appears as something produced, secondary, something which has come into being, a community produced by the labourer himself. It is clear that where ownership of the instrument is the relationship to the conditions of labour as property, in actual labour the instrument appears merely as *a means of individual labour*, and the art of really appropriating the instrument, to employ it as a means of labour, appears as a special skill of the labourer, which makes him the owner of his tools. In short, the essential character of gild or corporative systems (artisan labour as its subject and the constituent element of ownership)[1] is analysable in terms of a relation to the instrument of production: the tool as property. This differs from the relation to the earth, to the land as one's own, which is rather that of the raw material as property. In this historic state No. 2 property is thus constituted by the labouring subject's relation to this single element of the conditions of production, which makes him into a labouring proprietor; and this state may exist only as contradiction of state No. 1, or, if you like, as supplementary to a modified state No. 1. The first formula of capital negates this historic state also.

There is a third *possible form* which is to act as proprietor neither of the land nor of the instrument (i.e. nor of labour itself), but only of the means of subsistence, which are then found as the natural condition of the labouring subject. This is at bottom the formula of slavery and serfdom, which is also negated, or assumed to have been historically dissolved, in the relation of the worker to the conditions of production as capital.

The primitive forms of property necessarily dissolve into the relation of property to the different objective elements conditioning production; they are the economic basis of different forms of community, and in turn presuppose specific forms of community. These forms are significantly modified once labour itself is placed among the *objective conditions of production* (as in slavery and serfdom), as a result of which the simple

---

[1] The original text reads: *der handwerksmässigen Arbeit als ihr Subjekt, als Eigentuemer konstituierend.* This is not without possible ambiguities.

affirmative character of all forms of property embraced in No. 1 is lost and modified. All of these include potential slavery, and therefore their own abolition. So far as No. 2 is concerned, in which the particular kind of labour—i.e. its craft mastery and consequently property in the instrument of labour—equals property in the conditions of production, this admittedly excludes slavery and serfdom. However, it may lead to an analogous negative development in the form of a caste system.

The third form, of property in the means of subsistence, cannot contain any relationship of the *labouring* individual to the conditions of production, and therefore of existence, unless it is dissolved into slavery and serfdom. It can only be the relation of the member of the primitive community founded upon landed property, who happens to have lost his ownership of land without as yet having advanced to property No. 2, as in the case of the Roman plebs at the time of "bread and circuses".[1] The relation of retainers to their lords, or that of personal service, is essentially different. For it (personal service) forms at bottom merely the mode of existence of the landowner, who no longer labours himself, but whose property includes the labourers themselves as serfs, etc., among the conditions of production. What we have here as an essential relation of appropriation is the *relationship of domination*. Appropriation can create no such relation to animals, the soil, etc., even though the animal serves its master. The appropriation of another's *will* is presupposed in the relationship of domination. Beings without will, like animals, may indeed render services, but their owner is not thereby *lord and master*. However, what we see here is, how the *relations of domination and servitude* also enter into this formula of the appropriation of the instruments of production; and they

---

[1] *Translator's note:* i.e. of a propertyless mass living on a public dole.

constitute a necessary ferment of the development and decay of all primitive relations of property and production. At the same time they express their limitations. To be sure, they are also reproduced in capital, though in an indirect (mediated) form, and hence they also constitute a ferment in its dissolution, and are the emblems of its limitations.

* "The right to sell oneself and one's dependents in times of distress, was unfortunately general; it prevailed both in the North, among the Greeks and in Asia. The right of the creditor to take the defaulting debtor into servitude, and to redeem the debt either by his labour or by the sale of his person, was almost equally widespread" (Niebuhr, I, 600). [In another passage, Niebuhr explains the difficulties and misunderstandings of Greek writers of the Augustan period over the relationship between Patricians and Plebeians and their confusion of this relationship with that between Patrons and Clients, as being due to the fact that "they were writing at a time *when rich and poor constituted the only real classes of citizens;* where the man in need, no matter how noble his origins, required a Patron and the millionaire, even though only a freedman, was sought after as a Patron. They could find scarcely a trace of inherited relations of attachment". (I. 620)]. "Artisans were to be found in both classes (resident aliens and freedmen together with their descendants), and plebeians who abandoned agriculture passed into the limited citizen status enjoyed by these. Nor did they lack the honour of legally recognised gilds, and these were so highly respected that Numa was supposed to have been their founder. There were nine such gilds; pipers, goldsmiths, carpenters, dyers, harness-makers, tanners, saddlers, coppersmiths and potters, the ninth corporation embracing the rest of the crafts. . . . Those among them who were independent citizens, or who enjoyed a status equivalent to citizenship, independent of any patron (supposing such status was recognised); or those who were descendants of dependent men whose bond had lapsed with the extinction of their patrons' families: these undoubtedly remained as remote from the quarrels of ancient citizens and the commons (*der Gemeinde*) as the Florentine gilds remained outside the feuds of the Guelf and Ghibelline families. It is probable that the population in servitude were still as a whole at the disposal of the patricians (I, 623).

* On the one hand we presuppose historical processes which transform a mass of individuals of a nation, if not perhaps immediately into genuine free labourers, then at any rate into potential free labourers, whose only property is their labour-power and the possibility of exchanging it for the existing values. Such individuals confront all objective conditions of production as *alien property*, as their own *non-property*, but at the same time as something which can be exchanged as *values* and therefore to some extent appropriated by living labour. Such historic processes of dissolution are the following: the dissolution of the servile relationship which binds the labourer to the soil, and to the lord of the soil, but in fact assumes his property in the means of subsistence (which amounts in truth to his separation from the soil); the dissolution of relations of property which constitute a labourer as yeoman, or free, working, petty landowner or tenant (colonus), or free peasant;[1] the dissolution of gild relations which presuppose the labourer's property in the instrument of production and labour itself, as a certain form of craft skill[2] not merely as the source of property but as property itself; also the dissolution of the relation of clientship in its different types, in which *non-proprietors* appear as co-consumers of the surplus produce in the

[1] *Note by Marx:* We take for granted the dissolution of the even more ancient forms of communal property and real community.
[2] *handwerksmässig bestimmte Geschicklichkeit.*

retinue of their lord, and in return wear his livery, take part in his feuds, perform real or imaginary acts of personal service, etc. Closer analysis will show that what is dissolved in all these processes of dissolution are relations of production in which use-value predominates; production for immediate use. Exchange-value and its production presuppose the predominance of the other form. Thus in all the above circumstances deliveries in kind and labour services (*Naturaldienste*), predominate over money payments and services remunerated by money. But this is only incidental.[1] Again, closer examination will also reveal that all the dissolved relations were rendered possible only by a certain degree of development of the material (and therefore also of the mental) productive forces.

* What concerns us at this point is the following. The process of dissolution which turns a mass of individuals in a nation, etc., into potential free wage-labourers—individuals obliged merely by their lack of property to labour and to sell their labour—does *not* presuppose the *disappearance* of the previous sources of income or (in part) of the previous conditions of property of these individuals. On the contrary, it assumes that *only* their use has been altered, that their mode of existence has been transformed, that they have passed into other people's hands as a *free fund*, or perhaps that they have partly remained in *the same hands*. But this much is evident. The process which has in one way or another separated a mass of individuals from its previous affirmative relations to the *objective conditions of labour*, which negated these relations and thereby transformed these individuals into *free labourers*, is also the same process which has liberated these *objective conditions of labour* potentially from *their previous ties* to the individuals which are now separated from them. (These conditions of labour

1 Marx's phrase may also be read as meaning: "But this observation is by the way."

comprise land, raw material, means of subsistence, instruments of labour, money or all of these.) They are still *present*, but present in a different form, as a *free fund*, one in which all the old political, etc., relations are obliterated, and which now confront those separated, propertyless individuals merely in the form of *values*, of values maintaining themselves and each other.[1] The same process which counterposes the masses of free labourers to the *objective conditions of labour*, has also counterposed these conditions to them as *capital*. The historic process was one of the separation of hitherto combined elements; its result is therefore not the disappearance of one of these elements, but a situation in which each of them appears negatively related to the other: the (potentially) free labourer on one hand, (potential) capital on the other. The separation of the objective conditions from the classes which are now transformed into free labourers, must equally appear at the opposite pole as the establishment of independence by these very conditions.

* Let us consider the relationship of capital and wage labour not as something which has already reached decisive importance, and encroaches on production as a whole,[2] but as something which is still in the process of historic formation. We consider the original transformation of money into capital, the process of exchange between capital existing only potentially on one hand, and the free labourers existing potentially on the other. We then find ourselves naturally making the simple observation, with which the economists make great play—namely, that the side which appears as capital must possess raw materials, tools and food enough to enable the worker to live

---

[1] *an sich festhaltenden Werten.*

[2] *Marx's note :* For in this case capital, presupposed as the condition of wage-labour, is the product of labour, and established as condition by labour itself, created by labour as its own presupposition,

before production is completed. Moreover, it would appear that accumulation—an accumulation prior to labour and not arising from labour—must have taken place on the part of the capitalist, which enables him to set the labourer to work and to maintain him in activity, as living labour power.[1] This action of capital, which is independent and not established by labour, is then transferred from this history of its origin into the present, and transformed into a factor of its reality and effectiveness, of its self-creation (*Selbstformation*). Finally, the eternal right of capital to the fruit of other men's labour is derived from this state of affairs, or rather what happens is, that the mode of acquisition of capital is derived from the simple and "just" laws of the exchange of equivalents.

* Wealth occurring in the form of money can only be realised against the objective conditions of labour, because and if these have been separated from labour itself. We have seen that money can in part be accumulated by the sheer exchange of equivalents; however, this is so insignificant a source that it is not worth mention historically—assuming, that is, that we suppose this money to have been earned by the exchange of one's own labour. It is rather money accumulated by usury—especially usury on landed property—and mobile (monetary) wealth accumulated through mercantile profits, that turns into capital in the strict sense, into industrial capital. We will have

---

[1] *Marx's note:* Once capital and wage labour have been established as their own prerequisites, i.e. as a base presupposed for production, the following state of affairs appears to exist: In the first instance it seems that the capitalist must possess not only a fund of raw materials and means of subsistence sufficient for the labourer to reproduce himself, to produce the necessary means of subsistence, to realise *necessary labour;* but also a fund of raw material and instruments of production, by means of which the labourer realises his surplus labour, i.e. the capitalist's profit. Further analysis will reveal that the labourer is constantly creating a double fund for the capitalist, or in the form of capital. One part of this fund constantly fulfils the conditions of his own existence, the other part, the conditions of existence of capital. As we have seen, surplus capital—and surplus capital in its relation to its prehistoric relation to labour—includes the *appropriation* of all *real, present capital,* and of each element of such capital, which is appropriated uniformly as *alien labour* transformed into an object and appropriated by capital, without exchange, without the transfer of an equivalent for it.

occasion to deal with both forms below—that is, in so far as they themselves appear not as forms of capital but as prior forms of wealth which are the prerequisites for capital.

* As we have seen the concept—the origin—of capital implies *money* as its starting-point, and therefore it implies the existence of wealth in the form of money. It equally implies a derivation from circulation; capital appears as the *product* of circulation. Capital formation does not therefore arise from landed property (though it might arise from the agricultural tenant in so far as he is also a trader in farm products), nor from the gild (though this also provides a possibility) but from mercantile and usurious wealth. But the merchant and usurer only encounter the conditions which permit the purchase of free labour, once free labour has been detached from the objective conditions of its existence as a result of a historical process. At this point it also becomes possible to buy these *conditions* themselves. Under gild conditions, for instance, mere money (unless it is the money of gild masters) cannot purchase looms in order to put men to work on them; there are regulations determining how many looms a man may employ, etc. In short, the instrument of labour is still so intimately merged with living labour, appearing as the domain of living labour, that it does not truly circulate. What enables monetary wealth to turn into capital is, on the one hand, that it finds free labourers, and on the other, it finds means of subsistence, materials, etc., which would otherwise be in one form or another the *property* of the now objectiveless masses, and are also *free* and available for sale.

However, the other condition of labour—a certain craft skill, the existence of the instrument as a means of labour, etc.—is found *ready to hand* by capital in this preparatory or first period of capital. This is partly the result of the urban gild system, partly of domestic industry, or such industry as exists as an accessory to agriculture. The historic process is not the result of capital, but its prerequisite. By means of this process the capitalist then inserts himself as a (historical) middleman between landed property, or between any kind of property, and labour. History ignores the sentimental illusions about capitalist and labourer forming an association, etc.; nor is there a trace of such illusions in the development of the concept of capital. Sporadically, *manufacture* may develop locally in a framework belonging to quite a different period, as in the Italian cities *side by side* with the gilds. But if capital is to be the generally dominant form of an epoch, its conditions must be developed not merely locally, but on a large scale. (This is compatible with the possibility that during the dissolution of the gilds individual gild-masters may turn into industrial capitalists; however, in the nature of the phenomenon, this happens rarely. All in all, the entire gild system—both master and journeyman—dies out, where the capitalist and the labourer emerge.)

 * However, it is evident, and borne out by closer analysis of the historic epoch which we are now discussing, that the *age of dissolution* of the earlier modes of production and relations of the worker to the objective conditions of labour, is *simultaneously an age* in which *monetary wealth* has already developed to a certain extent, and also one in which it is rapidly growing and expanding, by means of the circumstances which accelerate this dissolution. Just as it is itself an agent of that dissolution, so that dissolution is the condition of its transformation into capital. But the *mere existence of monetary wealth*, even its conquest of a sort of supremacy, is not sufficient for this *dissolution to result in capital*. If it were, then ancient Rome, Byzantium, etc., would have concluded their history with free labour and capital, or rather, would have

entered upon a new history. There the dissolution of the old relations of property was also tied to the development of monetary wealth—of commerce, etc. However, in fact the result of this dissolution was not industry, but the domination of countryside over city.

The *original formation of capital* does not, as is often supposed, proceed by the *accumulation* of food, tools, raw materials or in short, of the *objective* conditions of labour detached from the soil and already fused with human labour.[1] Not by means of capital creating the objective conditions of labour. Its *original formation* occurs simply because the historic process of the dissolution of an old mode of production, allows value, existing in the form of *monetary wealth* to *buy* the objective conditions of labour on one hand, to exchange the *living* labour of the now free workers for money, on the other. All these elements are already in existence. What separates them out is a historic process, a process of dissolution, and it is *this* which enables money to turn into *capital*. In so far as money itself plays a part here, it is only to the extent that it is itself an extremely powerful agent of dissolution which intervenes in the process, and hence contributes to the creation of the *plucked*, objective-less, *free labourers*, It is certainly not by *creating* the objective conditions of such labourers' existence, but rather by accelerating their separation from them, i.e. by accelerating their loss of property.

For instance, when the great English landowners dismissed their retainers, who had consumed a share

[1] *Marx's note:* Nothing is more obviously and superficially circular than the reasoning which argues (a) that the *workers* who must be employed by capital if capital is to exist as such, must first be *created* and called into life by *its* accumulation (waiting, as it were, on its "Let there be labour"); while (b) capital could not *accumulate* without alien labour, except perhaps *its own labour*. I.e. that capital might itself exist in the form of *non-capital* and *non-money*, for prior to the existence of capital, labour can only realise its value in the form of handicraft work, of petty agriculture, etc.; in short, of forms, all of which permit little or *no accumulation*, allow for only a small surplus produce, and *consume* the greater part of that. We shall have to return to the concept of "accumulation" later.

of their surplus produce of their land; when their farmers drove out the small cottagers, etc., then a doubly free mass of living labour power was thrown on to the *labour market*: free from the old relation of clientship, villeinage or service, but also free from all goods and chattels, from every real and objective form of existence, *free from all property*. Such a mass would be reduced either to the sale of its labour power or to beggary, vagabondage or robbery as its only source of income. History records the fact that it first tried beggary, vagabondage and crime, but was herded off this road on to the narrow path which led to the labour market by means of gallows, pillory and whip. (Hence the *governments* of Henry VII, VIII, etc., also appear as conditions of the historic process of dissolution and as creators of the conditions for the existence of capital.) Conversely, the means of subsistence formerly consumed by the lords and their retainers, were now available for purchase by money, and money wished to purchase them in order through their instrumentality to purchase labour. Money had neither *created* nor *accumulated* these means of subsistence. They were already present, consumed and reproduced, before they were consumed and reproduced through the intervention of money. The only change was, that these means of production were now thrown on to the *exchange-market*. They had now been detached from their immediate connection with the mouths of the retainers, etc., and transformed from use-values into exchange-values, thus falling under the government and sovereignty of monetary wealth. The same applies to the instruments of labour. Monetary wealth neither invented nor manufactured spinning wheel and loom. But once spinners and weavers had been separated from their land, they and their wheels and looms came under the sway of monetary wealth, etc. *Capital unites the masses of hands and instruments which are already there.*

This and only this is what characterises it. It brings them together under its sway. This is its *real accumulation*; the accumulation of labourers plus their instruments at given points. We shall have to go into this more deeply when we come to the so-called accumulation of capital.

Admittedly, monetary wealth in the form of merchants' wealth had helped to accelerate and dissolve the old relations of production, and had, e.g., enabled the landowner to exchange his corn, cattle, etc., for imported use-values, instead of squandering his own production with his retainers, whose number, indeed, was to a large extent taken as the measure of his wealth. (This point has already been neatly made by A. Smith.) Monetary wealth had given greater significance to the exchange-value' of his revenue. This was also true of his tenants, who were already semi-capitalists, though in a rather disguised manner. The evolution of exchange-value is favoured by the existence of *money* in the form of a social order of merchants. It dissolves a production whose object is primarily immediate use-value, and the forms of property which correspond to such production—the relations of labour to its objective conditions—thus giving an impetus to the creation of a *labour market* (not to be confused with a slave market). However, even this effect of money is possible only if we presuppose the existence of *urban craft activity*, which rests *not* on capital and wage-labour, but on the organisation of labour in gilds, etc. Urban labour itself had created the means of production, for which the gilds became as great an embarrassment as were the old relations of landed property in an improved agriculture, which was in turn partly the consequence of the greater sale of agricultural products to the cities, etc.

Other circumstances assisted the dissolution of the old relations of production, accelerated the separation of the labourer or the non-labourer capable of work, from the objective conditions of his reproduction, and thus advanced the transformation of money into capital. Such were, e.g., the factors which in the sixteenth century increased the mass of commodities in circulation, the mass of currency in circulation, creating new needs and consequently raising the exchange value of native products, raising prices, etc. Nothing can therefore be more foolish than to conceive the *original formation* of capital as if it meant the accumulation and creation of the *objective conditions of production*—food, raw materials, instruments—which were then offered to the *dispossessed* workers. What happened was rather that monetary wealth partly helped to detach the labour power of the individuals capable of work, from these conditions. The rest of this process of separation proceeded without the intervention of monetary wealth. Once the original formation of capital had reached a certain level, monetary wealth could insert itself as an intermediary between the objective conditions of life, now "liberated" and the equally liberated, but now also *unfettered and footloose*, living labour powers, buying the one with the other. As to the *formation of monetary wealth* itself, before its transformation into capital: this belongs to the pre-history of the bourgeois economy. Usury, trade, the cities and government finance which arise with them, play the chief parts in it. Also *hoarding* by tenant farmers, peasants, etc., though to a smaller extent.

Trade is everywhere the intermediary for exchange value, or alternatively, the transfer of exchange value can be described as trade—for just as circulation acquires an independent existence in commerce, so does money in the social stratum of the merchants. We may see that the development of exchange and exchange-value brings about both the dissolution of *labour's relations of property in its* conditions of existence and also of *labour as something which is itself part of the objective conditions of production.* All these are relations which express both a predominance of use-value and of production directed towards immediate consumption, and also the predominance of a real community which is still present as an immediate prerequisite of production. Production based on exchange-value and a community based on the exchange of these exchange-values, and labour as the general condition of wealth, all presuppose and produce the separation of labour from its objective conditions. Though, as we saw in the last chapter on money, production for exchange and community based on exchange may appear to posit property as deriving solely from *labour,* and private property in the product of one's own labour as a precondition, this appearance is deceptive. The exchange of equivalents occurs (but it is merely) the surface layer of a production which rests on the appropriation of other people's labour *without exchange,* but under the *guise of exchange.* This system of exchange has *capital* as its basis. If we consider it in isolation from capital, as it appears on the surface, as an *independent* system, this is mere *illusion,* though a *necessary illusion.* It is therefore no longer surprising to find that the system of exchange-values—the exchange of equivalents measured in labour—turns into the *appropriation of other people's labour without exchange,* the total separation of labour and property, or rather that it reveals this appropriation as its concealed background. For the rule of exchange-values, and of production producing exchange-values *presupposes* alien labour power as itself an exchange-value. I.e. it presupposes the separation of living labour power from its objective conditions; a relationship to these—or to its own objectivity—as someone else's property; in a word, a relation to them as *capital.*

The golden age of labour emancipating itself, occurred only in those periods when feudalism was in decay, but still engaged in internecine conflict, as in England in the fourteenth and the first half of the fifteenth centuries. If labour is once again to be related to its objective conditions as to its property, another system must replace that of private exchange, for as we have seen private exchange assumes the exchange of labour transformed into objects against labour-power, and thereby the appropriation of living labour without exchange.

Historically, money is often transformed into capital in quite simple and obvious ways. Thus, the merchant sets to work a number of spinners and weavers, who formerly engaged in these activities as subsidiary occupations to their agricultural work, and turns a subsidiary occupation into a principal one, after which he has them under his control and sway as wage-labourers. The next step is to remove them from their homes and to assemble them in a single house of labour. In this simple process it is evident that the merchant has prepared neither raw materials nor instruments nor means of subsistence for the weaver or the spinner. All he has done is gradually to confine them to one sort of labour, in which they are dependent on the *buyer*, the *merchant*, and thus eventually find themselves producing solely *for* and *by means of* him. Originally he has bought their labour merely by the purchase of their product. As soon as they confine themselves to the production of this exchange-value, and are therefore obliged to produce immediate *exchange-values*, and to exchange their labour entirely for money in order to go on living, they come under his domination. Finally, even the illusion of *selling* him their products, disappears. He purchases their labour and takes away first their property in the product, soon also their ownership of the instrument, unless he allows them the *illusion of ownership* in order to diminish his costs of production.

The original historical forms in which capital appears at first sporadically or *locally*, *side by side* with the old modes of production, but gradually bursting them asunder, make up *manufacture* in the proper sense of the word (not yet the factory). This arises, where there is mass-production for export—hence on the *basis of large-scale maritime and overland trade*, and in the centres of such trade, as in the Italian cities, Constantinople, the Flemish, Dutch cities, some Spanish ones such as Barcelona, etc. Manufacture does not initially capture the so-called *urban crafts*, but the *rural subsidiary occupations*, spinning and weaving, the sort of work which least requires craft skill, technical training. Apart from those great emporia, in which it finds the basis of an *export* market, and where production is, as it were *by its spontaneous nature*, directed towards exchange-value—i.e. manufactures directly connected with shipping, including shipbuilding itself, etc.—manufacture first establishes itself not in the cities but in the countryside, in villages lacking gilds, etc. The rural subsidiary occupations contain the broad basis of manufactures, whereas a high degree of progress in production is required in order to carry on the urban crafts as factory industries. Such branches of production as glassworks, metal factories, sawmills, etc., which from the start demand a greater concentration of labour-power, utilise more natural power, and demand both mass-production and a concentration of the means of production, etc.: these also lend themselves to manufacture. Similarly paper-mills, etc.

The other aspect of this process is the appearance of the tenant farmer and the transformation of the agricultural population into free day-labourers. Though the last place where this transformation triumphs in its purest and most logical forms, is the countryside, some of its earliest developments occur there. Hence the ancients, who never advanced beyond specifically urban craft skill and application, were never able to achieve large-scale industry. For its first prerequisite is the involvement of the entire countryside in the production, not of use values, but of exchange values. Glassworks, papermills, ironworks, etc. cannot be conducted on gild principles. They require mass-production, sales to a general market, *monetary wealth* on the part of the entrepreneur. Not that he creates the subjective or objective conditions; but under the old relations of property and production these conditions cannot be brought together. (After this the dissolution of the relations of serfdom and the rise of manufacture gradually transform all branches of production into branches operated by capital.) However, the towns themselves contain an element for the formation of genuine wage-labour—namely, day-labourers outside the gild system, unskilled labourers, etc.

* We thus see that the transformation of money into capital presupposes a historic process which separates the objective conditions of labour, and makes them independent of and sets them against the labourers. However, once capital and its process have come into being, they conquer all production and everywhere bring about and accentuate the separation between labour and property, labour and the objective conditions of labour. Subsequent development will show[1] in what ways capital destroys artisan labour, small working landownership, etc., and also itself in those forms in which it does *not* appear in contradiction to labour: *petty capital*, and intermediate or hybrid types between the classic, adequate mode of production of capital itself, and the old modes of production (in their original form), or as renewed on the basis of capital.

* The only accumulation which is a prerequisite for the rise of capital, is that of *monetary wealth*, which, when considered in isolation, is entirely unproductive,

[1] The passage could also mean: "We shall see later."

emerges only from circulation and belongs only to circulation. Capital rapidly creates itself an internal market by destroying all rural subsidiary crafts, i.e. by spinning and weaving for all, providing clothing for all, etc.; in short by turning the commodities formerly produced as immediate use-values into exchange-values. This process is the automatic result of the separation of the labourers from the soil and from their property (though even only serf property) in the conditions of production.

* Though urban crafts are based substantially on exchange and the creation of exchange-values, the main object of production is not *enrichment* or *exchange-value as exchange-value*, but the *subsistence of man as an artisan, as a master-craftsman*, and consequently use-value. Production is therefore everywhere subordinate to a presupposed consumption, supply to demand, and its expansion is slow.

* *The production of capitalists and wage-labourers is therefore a major product of the process by which capital turns itself into values.* Ordinary political economy, which concentrates only on the objects produced, forgets this entirely. Inasmuch as this process establishes reified labour as what is simultaneously the *non-reification* of the labourer, as the reification of a subjectivity opposed to the labourer, as the *property* of someone else's will, capital is necessarily also a *capitalist*. The idea of some socialists, that we need capital but not capitalists, is completely false. The concept of capital implies that the objective conditions of labour—and these are its own product—acquire a *personality* as against labour, or what amounts to the same thing, that they are established as the property of a personality other than the worker's. The concept of capital implies the capitalist. However, this error is certainly no greater than that of, e.g., all philologists who speak of the existence of *capital* in classical

antiquity, and of Roman or Greek capitalists. This is merely another way of saying that in Rome and Greece labour was *free*, an assertion which these gentlemen would hardly make. If we now talk of plantation-owners in America as capitalists, if they *are* capitalists, this is due to the fact that they exist as anomalies within a world market based upon free labour. Were the term capital to be applicable to classical antiquity[1]—though the word does not actually occur among the ancients[2]—then the nomadic hordes with their flocks on the steppes of Central Asia would be the greatest capitalists, for the original meaning of the word capital is cattle. Hence the contract of *metairie* (crop-sharing) which is frequent in the South of France, because of capital shortage, is still sometimes called '*bail de bestes à cheptel*' (contract of leasing cattle).[3] If we permit ourselves a little bad Latin, then our capitalists or *Capitales Homines* (headmen) would be those "*qui debent censum de capite*" (who pay a head tax.)

* Difficulties which do not arise in the conceptual analysis of money do arise in that of capital. Capital is essentially a *capitalist*; but at the same time production in general is *capital*, as an element in the existence of the capitalist quite distinct from him. Thus we shall later find that in the term *capital* much is subsumed that does not apparently belong to the concept. E.g. capital is loaned. It is accumulated, etc. In all these relations it appears to be a mere object, and entirely to coincide with the matter of which it consists. However, further analysis will clarify this and other problems. (In passing, the following amusing observation: The good Adam Mueller, who takes all figurative phrases in a

[1] Marx's condensed phrase is merely "If we are to talk of capital" and probably requires this amplification.

[2] *Marx's note*: "But among the Greeks the word *arkhais* is used for what the Romans called the *principalis summa reicreditae* (the principal of a loan)."

[3] Marx: *grad ausnahmsweis*. It is not clear whether this means that the contract is exceptional, or that its description in these terms is exceptional.

mystical sense, had also heard about *living capital* in ordinary life, as opposed to *dead* capital, and dresses up the notion theosophically. King Athelstan could have taught him a thing or two about this: "Reddam de meo proprio decimas Deo tam in *Vivente Capitale* quam in *mortuis fructuis terrae.*" (I shall give a tithe of my property to God, both in living cattle and in the dead fruits of the soil.)) Money always retains the same form in the same substratum, and is therefore more readily conceived as an object. But the same thing, commodity, money, etc., can represent capital or revenue, etc. Thus even the economists recognise that money is nothing tangible, but that the same thing can be subsumed now under the heading capital, now under some other and quite contrary term, and accordingly that it *is* or *is not* capital. It is evidently *a relation and can only be a relation of production.*

Supplementary Texts of Marx and Engels on Problems of Historical Periodisation

FROM "THE GERMAN IDEOLOGY"
(PART I)

(A)

THE way in which men produce their means of subsistence depends first of all on the nature of the actual means they find in existence and have to reproduce. This mode of production must not be considered simply as being the reproduction of the physical existence of the individuals. Rather it is a definite form of activity of these individuals, a definite form of expressing their life, a definite *mode of life* on their part. As individuals express their life, so they are. What they are, therefore, coincides with their production, both with *what* they produce and with *how* they produce. The nature of individuals thus depends on the material conditions determining their production.

This production only makes its appearance with the increase of population. In its turn this presupposes the intercourse of individuals with one another. The form of this intercourse is again determined by production.

The relations of different nations among themselves depend upon the extent to which each has developed its productive forces, the division of labour and internal intercourse. This statement is generally recognised. But not only the relation of one nation to others, but also the whole internal structure of the nation itself depends on the stage of development reached by its production and its internal and external intercourse. How far the productive forces of a nation are developed is shown most manifestly by the degree to which the division of labour has been carried. Each new productive force, in so far as it is not merely a quantitative extension of productive forces already known (for instance the bringing into cultivation of fresh land), brings about a further development of the division of labour.

The division of labour inside a nation leads at first to the separation of industrial and commercial from agricultural labour, and hence to the separation of town and country and a clash of interests between them. Its further development leads to the separation of commercial from industrial labour. At the same time through the division of labour there develop further, inside these various branches, various divisions among the individuals co-operating in definite kinds of labour. The relative position of these individual groups is determined by the methods employed in agriculture, industry and commerce (patriarchalism, slavery, estates, classes). These same conditions are to be seen (given a more developed intercourse) in the relations of different nations to one another.

The various stages of development in the division of labour are just so many different forms of ownership; i.e. the existing stage in the division of labour determines also the relations of individuals to one another with reference to the material, instrument, and product of labour.

The first form of ownership is tribal ownership. It corresponds to the undeveloped stage of production, at which a people lives by hunting and fishing, by the rearing of beasts or, in the highest stage, agriculture. In the latter case it presupposes a great mass of uncultivated stretches of land. The division of labour is at this stage still very elementary and is confined to a further extension of the natural division of labour imposed by the family. The social structure is therefore limited to an extension of the family; patriarchal family chieftains; below them the members of the tribe; finally slaves. The slavery latent in the family only develops gradually with the increase of population, the growth of wants, and with the extension of external relations, of war or of trade.

The second form is the ancient communal and State ownership which proceeds especially from the union of several tribes into a city by agreement or by conquest, and which is still accompanied by slavery. Beside communal ownership we already find movable, and later also immovable, private property developing, but as an abnormal form subordinate to communal ownership. It is only as a community that the citizens hold power over their labouring slaves, and on this account alone, therefore, they are bound to the form of communal ownership. It is the communal private property which compels the active citizens to remain in this natural form of association over against their slaves. For this reason the whole structure of society based on this communal ownership, and with it the power of the people, decays in the same measure as immovable private property evolves. The division of labour is already more developed. We already find the antagonism of town and country; later the antagonism between those states which represent town interests and those which represent country, and inside the towns themselves the antagonism between industry and maritime commerce. The class relation between citizens and slaves is now completely developed.

This whole interpretation of history appears to be contradicted by the fact of conquest. Up till now violence, war, pillage, rape and slaughter, etc., have been accepted as the driving force of history. Here we must limit ourselves to the chief points and take therefore only a striking example—the destruction of an old civilisation by a barbarous people and the resulting formation of an entirely new organisation of society

(Rome and the barbarians; Feudalism and Gaul; the Byzantine Empire and the Turks). With the conquering barbarian people war itself is still, as hinted above, a regular form of intercourse, which is the more eagerly exploited as the population increases, involving the necessity of new means of production to supersede the traditional and, for it, the only possible, crude mode of production. In Italy it was, however, otherwise. The concentration of landed property (caused not only by buying up and indebtedness, but also by inheritance, since loose living being rife and marriage rare, the old families died out and their possessions fell into the hands of a few) and its conversion into grazing-land (caused not only by economic forces still operative to-day but by the importation of plundered and tribute-corn and the resultant lack of demand for Italian corn) brought about the almost total disappearance of the free population. The very slaves died out again and again, and had constantly to be replaced by new ones. Slavery remained the basis of the whole productive system. The plebeians, mid-way between freemen and slaves, never succeeded in becoming more than a proletarian rabble. Rome indeed never became more than a city; its connection with the provinces was almost exclusively political and could therefore easily be broken again by political events.

With the development of private property, we find here for the first time the same conditions which we shall find again, only on a more extensive scale, with modern private property. On the one hand the concentration of private property, which began very early in Rome (as the Licinian agrarian law proves), and proceeded very rapidly from the time of the civil wars and especially under the Emperors; on the other hand, coupled with this, the transformation of the plebeian small peasantry into a proletariat, which, however, owing to its intermediate position between propertied citizens and slaves, never achieved an independent development.

The third form of ownership is feudal or estate-property. If antiquity started out from the town and its little territory, the Middle Ages started out from the country. This different starting-point was determined by the sparseness of the population at that time, which was scattered over a large area and which received no large increase from the conquerors. In contrast to Greece and Rome, feudal development therefore extends over a much wider field, prepared by the Roman conquests and the spread of agriculture at first associated with it. The last centuries of the declining Roman Empire and its conquest by the barbarians destroyed a number of productive forces; agriculture had declined, industry had decayed for want of a market, trade had died out or been violently suspended, the rural and urban population had decreased. From these conditions and the mode of organisation of the conquest determined by them, feudal property developed under the influence of the Germanic military constitution. Like tribal and communal ownership, it is based again on a community; but the directly producing class standing over against it is not, as in the case of the ancient community, the slaves, but the enserfed small peasantry. As soon as feudalism is fully developed, there also arises antagonism to the towns. The hierarchical system of land ownership, and the armed bodies of retainers associated with it, gave the nobility power over the serfs. This feudal organisation was just as much as the ancient communal ownership, an association against a subjected producing class; but the form of association and the relation to the direct producers were different because of the different conditions of production

This feudal organisation of land-ownership had its counterpart in the towns in the shape of corporative property, the feudal organisation of trades. Here property consisted chiefly in the labour of each individual person. The necessity for association against the organised robber-nobility, the need for communal covered markets in an age when the industrialist was at the same time a merchant, the growing competition of the escaped serfs swarming into the rising towns, the feudal structure of the whole country: these combined to bring about the gilds. Further, the gradually accumulated capital of individual craftsmen and their stable numbers, as against the growing population, evolved the relation of journeyman and apprentice, which brought into being in the towns a hierarchy similar to that in the country.

Thus the chief form of property during the feudal epoch consisted on the one hand of landed property with serf-labour chained to it, and on the other of individual labour with small capital commanding the labour of journeymen. The organisation of both was determined by the restricted conditions of production —the small-scale and primitive cultivation of the land, and the craft type of industry. There was little division of labour in the heyday of feudalism. Each land bore in itself the conflict of town and country and the division into estates was certainly strongly marked; but apart from the differentiation of princes, nobility, clergy and peasants in the country, and masters, journeymen, apprentices and soon also the rabble of casual labourers in the towns, no division of importance took place. In agriculture it was rendered difficult by the strip-system, beside which the cottage industry of the peasants themselves emerged as another factor. In industry there was no division of labour at all in the individual trades themselves, and very little between them. The separation of industry and commerce was found already in existence in older towns; in the newer it only developed later, when the towns entered into mutual relations.

The grouping of larger territories into feudal king-doms was a necessity for the landed nobility as for the towns. The organisation of the ruling class, the nobility, had, therefore, everywhere a monarch at its head.

(B)

The greatest division of material and mental labour is the separation of town and country. The antagonism between town and country begins with the transition from barbarism to civilisation, from tribe to State, from locality to nation, and runs through the whole history of civilisation to the present day (the Anti-Corn Law League). The existence of the town implies, at the same time, the necessity of administration, police, taxes, etc., in short, of the municipality, and thus of politics in general. Here first became manifest the division of the population into two great classes, which is directly based on the division of labour and on the instruments of production. The town already is in actual fact the concentration of the population, of the instruments of production, of capital, of pleasures, of needs, while the country demonstrates just the opposite fact, their isola-tion and separation. The antagonism of town and country can only exist as a result of private property. It is the most crass expression of the subjection of the individual under the division of labour, under a definite activity forced upon him—a subjection which makes one man into a restricted town-animal, the other into a restricted country-animal, and daily creates anew the conflict between their interests. Labour is here again the chief thing, power *over* individuals, and as long as the latter exists, private property must exist. The aboli-tion of the antagonism between town and country is one of the first conditions of communal life, a condition which again depends on a mass of material premises and which cannot be fulfilled by the mere will, as anyone can see at the first glance. (These conditions have still to be enumerated.) The separation of town and country can also be understood as the separation of capital and landed property, as the beginning of the existence and development of capital independent of landed property—the beginning of property having its basis only in labour and exchange.

In the towns which, in the Middle Ages, did not derive ready-made from an earlier period but were formed anew by the serfs who had become free, each man's own particular labour was his only property apart from the small capital he brought with him, consisting almost solely of the most necessary tools of his craft. The competition of serfs constantly escaping into the town, the constant war of the country against the town and thus the necessity of an organised municipal military force, the bond of common ownership in a particular piece of work, the necessity of common buildings for the sale of their wares at a time when craftsmen were at the same time traders, and the consequent exclusion of the unauthorised from these buildings, the conflict among the interests of the various crafts, the necessity of protecting their laboriously acquired skill, and the feudal organisation of the whole of the country: these were the causes of the union of the workers of each craft in gilds. We have not at this point to go further into the manifold modifications of the gild system, which arise through later historical developments.

The flight of the serfs into the towns went on without interruption right through the Middle Ages. These serfs, persecuted by their lords in the country, came separately into the towns, where they found an organised community, against which they were powerless, in which they had to subject themselves to the station assigned to them by the demand for their labour and the interest of their organised urban competitors. These

workers, entering separately, were never able to attain
to any power, since if their labour was of the gild type
which had to be learned, the gild-masters bent them
to their will and organised them according to their
interest; or if their labour was not such as had to be
learned, and therefore not of the gild type, they became day-labourers and never managed to organise,
remaining an unorganised rabble. The need for day-
labourers in the towns created the rabble. These towns
were true "associations", called forth by the direct need
of providing for the protection of property, and multi-
plying the means of production and defence of the
separate members. The rabble of these towns was
devoid of any power, composed as it was of individuals
strange to one another who had entered separately, and
who stood unorganised over against an organised
power, armed for war, and jealously watching over
them. The journeymen and apprentices were organised
in each craft as it best suited the interest of the masters.
The filial relationship in which they stood to their
masters gave the latter a double power—on the one
hand because of their influence on the whole life of the
journeymen, and on the other because, for the journeymen who worked with the same master, it was a real
bond, which held them together against the journeymen of other masters and separated them from these.
And finally, the journeymen were bound to the existing
order by their simple interest in becoming masters
themselves. While, therefore, the rabble at least carried
out revolts against the whole municipal order, revolts
which remained completely ineffective because of their
powerlessness, the journeymen never got further than
small acts of insubordination within separate gilds,
such as belong to the very nature of the gild. The great
risings of the Middle Ages all radiated from the country,
but equally remained totally ineffective because of the
isolation and consequent crudity of the peasants.

In the towns, the division of labour between the individual gilds was as yet quite natural, and, in the gilds themselves, not at all developed between the individual workers. Every workman had to be versed in a whole round of tasks, had to be able to make everything that was to be made with his tools. The limited commerce and the scanty communication between the individual towns, the lack of population and the narrow needs did not allow of a higher division of labour, and therefore every man who wished to become a master had to be proficient in the whole of his craft. Thus there is found with medieval craftsmen an interest in their special work and in proficiency in it, which was capable of rising to a narrow artistic sense. For this very reason, however, every medieval craftsman was completely absorbed in his work, to which he had a contented, slavish relationship, and to which he was subjected to a far greater extent than the modern worker, whose work is a matter of indifference to him.

Capital in these towns was a natural capital, consisting of a house, the tools of the craft, and the natural, hereditary customers; and not being realisable, on account of the backwardness of commerce and the lack of circulation, it descended from father to son. Unlike modern capital, which can be assessed in money and which may be indifferently invested in this thing or that, this capital was directly connected with the particular work of the owner, inseparable from it and to this extent "estate" capital.

The next extension of the division of labour was the separation of production and commerce, the formation of a special class of merchants; a separation which, in the towns bequeathed by a former period, had been handed down (among other things with the Jews) and which very soon appeared in the newly formed ones. With this there was given the possibility of commercial communications transcending the immediate neighbourhood, a possibility, the realisation of which depended on the existing means of communication, the state of public safety in the countryside, which was determined by political conditions (during the whole of the Middle Ages, as is well known, the merchants travelled in armed caravans), and on the cruder or more advanced needs (determined by the stage of culture attained) of the region accessible to intercourse. With commerce the prerogative of a particular class, with the extension of trade through the merchants beyond the immediate surroundings of the town, there immediately appears a reciprocal action between production and commerce. The towns enter into relations *with one another*, new tools are brought from one town into the other, and the separation between production and commerce soon calls forth a new division of production between the individual towns, each of which is soon exploiting a predominant branch of industry. The local restrictions of earlier times begin gradually to be broken down.

In the Middle Ages the citizens in each town were compelled to unite against the landed nobility to save their skins. The extension of trade, the establishment of communications, led the separate towns to get to know other towns, which had asserted the same interests in the struggle with the same antagonist. Out of the many local corporations of burghers there arose only gradually the burgher *class*. The conditions of life of the individual burghers became, on account of their antagonism to the existing relationships and of the mode of labour determined by these, conditions which were common to them all and independent of each individual. The burghers had created the conditions in so far as they had torn themselves free from feudal ties, and were created by them in so far as they were determined by their antagonism to the feudal system which they found in existence. When the individual towns began to enter into associations, these common conditions developed into class conditions. The same conditions, the same antagonism, the same interests necessarily called forth on the whole similar customs everywhere. The bourgeoisie itself, with its conditions, develops only gradually, splits according to the division of labour into various factions and finally absorbs all earlier possessing classes (while it develops the majority of the earlier non-possessing, and a part of the earlier possessing, class into a new class, the proletariat) in the measure to which all earlier property is transformed into industrial or commercial capital. The separate individuals form a class only in so far as they have to carry on a common battle against another class; otherwise they are on hostile terms with each other as competitors. On the other hand, the class in its turn achieves an independent existence over against the individuals, so that the latter find their conditions of existence predestined, and hence have their position in life and their personal development assigned to them by their class, become subsumed under it. This is the same phenomenon as the subjection of the separate individuals to the division of labour and can only be removed by the abolition of private property and of labour itself. We have already indicated several times how this subsuming of individuals under the class brings with it their subjection to all kinds of ideas, etc.

It depends purely on the extension of commerce whether the productive forces achieved in a locality, especially inventions, are lost for later development or not. As long as there exists no commerce transcending the immediate neighbourhood, every invention must be made separately in each locality, and mere chances such as irruptions of barbaric peoples, even ordinary wars, are sufficient to cause a country with advanced productive forces and needs to have to start right over again from the beginning. In primitive history every invention had to be made daily anew and in each locality independently. How little highly developed productive forces are safe from complete destruction, given even a relatively very extensive commerce, is proved by the Phœnicians, whose inventions were for the most part lost for a long time to come through the ousting of this nation from commerce, its conquest by Alexander and its consequent decline. Likewise, for instance, glass-painting in the Middle Ages. Only when commerce has become world-commerce and has as its basis big industry, when all nations are drawn into the competitive struggle, is the permanence of the acquired productive forces assured.

The immediate consequence of the division of labour between the various towns was the rise of manufactures, branches of production which had outgrown the gild-system. Manufactures first flourished, in Italy and later in Flanders, under the historical premise of commerce with foreign nations. In other countries England and France for example, manufactures were at first confined to the home market. Besides the premises already mentioned manufactures depend on yet another: an already advanced concentration of population, particularly in the countryside, and of capital, which began to accumulate in the hands of individuals, partly in the gilds in spite of the gild regulations, partly among the merchants.

That labour which from the first presupposed a machine, even of the crudest sort, soon showed itself the most capable of development. Weaving, earlier carried on in the country by the peasants as a secondary occupation to procure their clothing, was the first labour to receive an impetus and a further development through the extension of commerce. Weaving was the first and remained the principal manufacture. The rising demand for clothing materials, consequent on the growth of population, the growing accumulation and mobilisation of natural capital through accelerated circulation, the demand for luxuries called forth by the latter and favoured generally by the gradual extension of commerce, gave weaving a quantitative and qualitative stimulus, which wrenched it out of the form of production hitherto existing. Alongside the peasants weaving for their own use, who continued with this sort of work, there emerged a new class of weavers in the towns, whose fabrics were destined for the whole home market and usually for foreign markets too. Weaving, an occupation demanding in most cases little skill and soon splitting up into countless branches, by its whole nature resisted the trammels of the gild. Weaving was therefore carried on mostly in villages and market-centres without gild organisation, which gradually became towns, and indeed the most flourishing towns in each land. With gild-free manufacture, property relations also quickly changed. The first advance beyond natural, estate-capital was provided by the rise of merchants whose capital was from the beginning movable, capital in the modern sense as far as one can speak of it, given the circumstances of those times. The second advance came with manufacture, which again made mobile a mass of natural capital, and altogether increased the mass of movable capital as against that of natural capital. At the same time, manufacture became a refuge of the peasants from the gilds which excluded them or paid them badly, just as earlier the gild-towns had served as a refuge for the peasants from the oppressive landed nobility.

Simultaneously with the beginning of manufactures there was a period of vagabondage caused by the decline of the feudal bodies of retainers, the disbanding of the swollen armies which had flocked to serve the kings against their vassals, the improvement of agriculture, and the transformation of great strips of tillage into pasture-land. From this alone it is clear how this vagabondage is strictly connected with the disintegration of the feudal system. As early as the thirteenth century we find isolated epochs of this kind, but only at the end of the fifteenth and beginning of the sixteenth does this vagabondage make a general and permanent appearance. These vagabonds, who were so numerous that Henry VIII of England had 72,000 of them hanged, were only prevailed upon to work with the greatest difficulty and through the most extreme necessity, and then only after long resistance. The rapid rise of manufacturers, particularly in England, absorbed them gradually. With the advent of manufactures, the various nations entered into a competitive relationship, the struggle for trade, which was fought out in wars, protective duties and prohibitions, whereas earlier the nations, in so far as they were connected at all, had carried on an inoffensive exchange with each other. Trade had from now on a political significance.

With manufacture was given simultaneously a changed relationship between worker and employer. In the gilds the patriarchal relationship between journeyman and master maintained itself; in manufacture its place was taken by the monetary relation between worker and capitalist—a relationship which in the countryside and in small towns retained a patriarchal tinge, but in the larger, the real manufacturing towns, quite early lost almost all patriarchal complexion.

Manufacture and the movement of production in general received an enormous impetus through the extension of commerce which came with the discovery of America and the sea-route to the East Indies. The new products imported thence, particularly the masses of gold and silver which came into circulation and totally changed the position of the classes towards one

another, dealing a hard blow to feudal landed property
and to the workers; the expeditions of adventurers,
colonisation, and above all the extension of markets
into a world-market, which had now become possible
and was daily becoming more and more a fact, called
forth a new phase of historical development, into which
in general we cannot here enter further. Through the
colonisation of the newly discovered countries the
commercial struggle of the nations amongst one another was given new fuel and accordingly greater
extension and animosity.

The expansion of trade and manufacture accelerated
the accumulation of movable capital, while in the gilds,
which were not stimulated to extend their production,
natural capital remained stationary or even declined.
Trade and manufacture created the big bourgeoisie,
in the gilds was concentrated the petty bourgeoisie,
which no longer was dominant in the towns as formerly,
but had to bow to the might of the great merchants and
manufacturers. Hence the decline of the gilds, as soon
as they came into contact with manufacture.

The material, commercial relations of nations took
on, in the epoch of which we have been speaking, two
different forms. At first the small quantity of gold and
silver in circulation involved the ban on the export of
these metals; and industry, for the most part imported
from abroad and made necessary by the need for
employing the growing urban population, could not do
without those privileges which could be granted not
only, of course, against home competition, but chiefly
against foreign. The local gild privilege was in these
original prohibitions extended over the whole nation.
Customs duties originated from the tributes exacted
by the feudal lords from merchants passing through
their territories, tributes later imposed likewise by the
towns, and which, with the rise of the modern states,
were the treasury's most obvious means of raising

money. The appearance of American gold and silver on the European markets, the gradual development of industry, the rapid expansion of trade and the consequent rise of the non-gild bourgeoisie and of money, gave these measures another significance. The State, which was daily less and less able to do without money, now retained the ban on the export of gold and silver out of fiscal considerations; the bourgeois, who had as their chief object the cornering of these masses of money which were hurled on to the market, were thoroughly content with this; privileges established earlier became a source of income for the government and were sold for money; in the customs legislation there appeared the export-duty, which, since it only placed a hindrance in the way of industry, had a purely fiscal aim.

The second period began in the middle of the seventeenth century and lasted almost to the end of the eighteenth. Commerce and navigation had expanded more rapidly then manufacture, which played a secondary role; the colonies were becoming considerable consumers; and after long struggles the separate nations shared out the opening world-market among themselves. This period begins with the Navigation Laws and colonial monopolies. The competition of the nations among themselves was excluded as far as possible by tariffs, prohibitions and treaties; and in the last resort the competitive struggle was carried on and decided by wars (especially naval wars). The mightiest maritime nation, the English, retained preponderance in trade and manufacture. Here, already, we find concentration on one country. Manufacture was all the time sheltered by protective duties in the home market, by monopolies in the colonial market, and abroad as much as possible by differential duties. The working-up of home-produced material was encouraged (wool and linen in England, silk in France), the export of home-produced raw material forbidden (wool in England), and that of imported material neglected or suppressed (cotton in England). The nation dominant in sea-trade and colonial power naturally secured for itself also the greatest quantitative and qualitative expansion of manufacture. Manufacture could not be carried on without protection, since, if the slightest change takes place in other countries, it can lose its market and be ruined; under reasonably favourable conditions it may easily be introduced into a country, but for this very reason can easily be destroyed. At the same time through the mode in which it is carried on, particularly in the eighteenth century, in the countryside, it is so interwoven with the vital relationships of a great mass of individuals, that no country dare jeopardise its existence by permitting free competition. In so far as it manages to export, it therefore depends entirely on the extension or restriction of commerce, and exercises a relatively very small reaction on the latter. Hence its secondary importance and the influence of the merchants in the eighteenth century. It was especially the merchants and shippers who more than anybody else pressed for State protection and monopolies; the manufacturers demanded and indeed received protection, but all the time were inferior in political importance to the merchants. The commercial towns, particularly the maritime towns, won to some extent the civilised outlook of the big bourgeoisie, but in the factory towns an extreme petty-bourgeois outlook persisted. Cf. Aikin, etc. The eighteenth century was the century of trade. Pinto says this expressly: "*Le commerce fait la marotte du siècle*," ("Commerce is the rage of the century"); and, "*depuis quelque temps il n'est plus question que de commerce, de navigation et de marine*" ("for some time now people have been talking only about commerce, navigation, and the navy").

This period is also characterised by the cessation of the bans on the export of gold and silver and the beginning of the bullion-trade; by banks, national debts, paper-money; by speculation in stocks and shares and stock-jobbing in all articles; by the development of finance in general. Again capital lost a great part of the natural character which had clung to it.

MARX TO ENGELS, MARCH 14, 1868

. . . INCIDENTALLY, at the Museum have among other things worked through old Maurer's . . . writings on *German, Mark, Village, etc. Constitution.* He demonstrates very fully that private property in land is of later origin, etc. Completely refutes the idiotic Westphalian Junker view (Möser, etc.) that the Germans settled individually and only subsequently formed villages, *Gaue,* etc. Interesting just at this moment, that the *Russian* practice of redistributing the land at fixed intervals (in Germany initially every year) survived in Germany here and there until the eighteenth and even the nineteenth century. Though M(aurer) knew nothing of the view I have put forward, namely that the Asian or Indian forms of property constitute the initial ones everywhere in Europe, he provides further proof of it. The Russians now lose even the last traces of a claim to originality, even in this line.[1] All that is left of them is, that they are still stuck in the forms which their neighbours have long since cast off. . . .

I learned from Maurer that the *Danes* initiated the revolution in the accepted views about the history and development of "Germanic" property, etc. Apparently they are tremendously active in all kinds of archaeology. However, though they provide the impulse, somewhere or else,[2] there's always some weakness. They lack the

[1] "Originality in this line" in English in the original text.
[2] "Somewhere or else" in English in the original text,

right critical instinct and above all, the sense of proportion. I was extremely struck by the fact that Maurer,
though often referring to Africa, Mexico, etc., for
purposes of illustration, knows absolutely nothing
about the Celts, and therefore ascribes the development
of landed property in France entirely to the German
conquerors. "As though"—as Herr Bruno would say
—"as though" we did not possess a Celtic (Welsh)
book of laws from the eleventh century which is
entirely communist, and "as though" the French had
not excavated original communities of the Celtic form
here and there, and precisely in recent years. "As
though"! But the explanation is quite simple. Old
Maurer studied only German and ancient Roman
conditions, and beyond these only oriental (Greco-
Turkish) ones.

MARX TO ENGELS, MARCH 25, 1868

With regard to Maurer. His books are exceptionally
important. Not only primitive times but the whole
later development of the free imperial cities, of the
immunity of landowners, of public authority and of the
struggle between free peasantry and serfdom is given
an entirely new form.

Human history is like palaeontology. Owing to a
certain judicial blindness even the best intelligences
absolutely fail to see the things which lie in front of
their noses. Later, when the moment has arrived, we
are surprised to find traces everywhere of what we failed
to see. The first reaction against the French Revolution
and the period of Enlightenment bound up with it
was naturally to see everything as medieval and
romantic, even people like Grimm are not free from
this. The second reaction is to look beyond the
Middle Ages into the primitive age of each nation,

and that corresponds to the socialist tendency, although these learned men have no idea that the two have any connection. They are therefore surprised to find what is newest in what is oldest—even equalitarians, to a degree which would have made Proudhon shudder.

To show how much we are all implicated in this judicial blindness: right in *my own* neighbourhood, on the *Hunsrücken*, the old Germanic system survived up till the *last few years*. I now remember my father talking to me about it from a lawyer's point of view. Another proof: Just as the geologists, even the best, like Cuvier, have expounded certain facts in a completely distorted way, so philologists of the force of a Grimm *mistranslated* the simplest Latin sentences because they were under the influence of Möser etc., (who, I remember, was enchanted that "liberty" never existed among the Germans but that *"Luft macht eigen"* [the air makes the serf][1]) and others. E.g. the well-known passage in Tacitus: *"arva per annos* mutant et *superest ager,"* which means, "they exchange the fields, *arva"* (by lot, hence also *sortes* [lot] in all the later law codes of the barbarians) "and the common land remains over" (*ager* as public land contrasted with *arva*)—is translated by Grimm, etc.: "they cultivate fresh fields every year and still there is always (uncultivated) land over !"

So too the passage: "Colunt *discreti ac diversi"* [their tillage is separate and scattered] is supposed to prove that from time immemorial the Germans carried on cultivation on individual farms like Westphalian *junkers.* But the same passage continues: *"Vicos locant* non in nostrum morem *connexis et cohaerantibus aedificiis*: suum quisque locum *spatio circumdat"* [they do not lay out their villages with buildings connected

---

[1] A medieval German saying meaning that merely because he lived and breathed the air on a certain spot a man was enslaved—a serf or bondsman tied to the soil. *Ed. Eng. ed.*

and joined together after our fashion: each surrounds his dwelling with a strip of land]; and primitive Germanic villages still exist here and there in Denmark in the form described. Obviously Scandinavia must become as important for German jurisprudence and economics as for German mythology. And only by starting from there shall we be able to decipher our past again. For the rest even Grimm, etc., find in Caesar that the Germans always settled as *Geschlechts-genossenschaften*[1] and not as individuals: *"gentibus* cognationibusque qui uno coiereant* " [according to clans and kindreds, who settled together].

But what would old Hegel say in the next world if he heard that the *general* [*Allgemeine*] in German and Norse means nothing but the common land [*Gemein-land*], and the *particular, Sundre, Besondere,* nothing but the separate property divided off from the common land? Here are the logical categories coming damn well out of "our intercourse" after all.

MARX TO ZASULICH, MARCH 8, 1881

From the Second Draft

... IN appropriating the positive results of the capitalist mode of production, (Russia) is capable of developing and transforming the archaic form of its village community, instead of destroying it. (I observe by the way, that the form of communist property in Russia is the most modern form of the archaic type, which in turn has passed through a number of evolutionary changes.)

The archaic or primary formation of our globe contains a number of strata of different ages, one superimposed on the other. Just so the archaic formation of society reveals a number of different types, which characterise different and successive epochs.

[1] *Geschlechtsgenossenschaft*—the *gens* or patriarchal joint family. *Ed. Eng. ed.*

The Russian village community belongs to the youngest type in this chain. Here the peasant cultivator already owns the house in which he lives and the garden belonging to it. Here we have the first dissolving element of the archaic formation, unknown to older types. On the other hand all these are based on blood relationships between the members of the community, while the type to which the Russian commune belongs, is already emancipated from these narrow bonds, and is thus capable of greater evolution. The isolation of the village communities, the lack of links between their lives, this locally bounded microcosm, is not everywhere an immanent characteristic of the last of the primitive types. However, wherever it does occur, it permits the emergence of a central despotism above the communities. It seems to me that in Russia the original isolation, caused by the vast extent of the territory, is easily to be eliminated, once the fetters imposed by the government will have been burst.

I now come to the crux of the question. We cannot overlook the fact that the archaic type, to which the Russian commune belongs, conceals an internal dualism, which may under certain historic circumstances lead to its ruin. Property in land is communal, but each peasant cultivates and manages his plot on his own account, in a way recalling the small peasant of the West. Common ownership, divided petty cultivation: this combination which was useful in remoter periods, becomes dangerous in ours. On one hand mobile property, an element which plays an increasing part even in agriculture, gradually leads to differentiation of wealth among the members of the community, and therefore makes it possible for a conflict of interests to arise, particularly under the fiscal pressure of the state. On the other hand the economic superiority of communal ownership, as the base of co-operative and combined labour, is lost. . . .

From the Third Draft

Primitive communities are not all cut to a single pattern. On the contrary, taken together they form a series of social groupings, differing both in type and in age, and marking successive phases of development. One of these types, now by general agreement called "the agricultural community" is the type of the *Russian community*. Its counterpart in the West is the *Germanic community*, which is of very recent date. In the time of Julius Caesar it was not yet in existence, and when the Germanic tribes conquered Italy, Gaul, Spain, etc., it no longer functioned. In Julius Caesar's era there was already an annual redivision of the cultivable fields among groups—the *gentes* and *tribes*—but not yet among the individual families of a community; probably cultivation was also in groups, communal. In Germanic territory itself a natural evolution has transformed this community of a more archaic type into the *agricultural community* as described by Tacitus. After this period we lose sight of it. It died unnoticed in the course of the interminable wars and migrations; perhaps its end was violent. However, its natural viability is demonstrated by two unquestionable facts. A few scattered examples of this kind have survived all the vicissitudes of the middle ages until our own day, e.g. in my native region round Treves. But what is most significant, we find the new community which sprang from this older one, bearing its stamp to such an extent that Maurer, who investigated the one, was able to reconstruct the other. The new community, in which the cultivable soil belongs to the peasants as *private property*, whereas woodlands, pastures, and waste still remain *common land*, was also introduced by the Germans into all conquered countries. Thanks to the characteristics it derived from its prototype, it remained throughout the Middle Ages the unique stronghold of popular liberty and popular life.

The "village community" also occurs in Asia, among the Afghans, etc., but it is everywhere the *very youngest type*, as it were the last word of the *archaic formation* of societies. . . .

As the last phase of the primitive formation of society, the agricultural community is at the same time a transitional phase to the secondary formation, i.e. transition from society based on common property to society based on private property. The secondary formation comprises, as you must understand, the series of societies based on slavery and serfdom.

But does this mean that the historic career of the agricultural community must inevitably lead to this result? Certainly not. The dualism within it permits of an alternative: either the property element in it will overcome the collective element, or the other way round. Everything depends on the historical environment in which it occurs.

ENGELS TO MARX, DECEMBER 15, 1882

ENCLOSED is the appendix on the *Mark*. Be so kind as to send it back on *Sunday*, so that I can revise it on Monday—I was not able to conclude the final revision to-day.

I consider the view expounded here regarding the conditions of the peasantry in the Middle Ages and the rise of a *second* serfdom after the middle of the fifteenth century as on the whole incontrovertible. I have been right through Maurer for all the relevant passages and find nearly all my assertions there, *supported, moreover, with evidence*, while alongside of them are exactly the opposite, but either unsupported by evidence or taken from a period which is *not* that in question at all. This particularly applies to *Fronhöfe* [lands liable to feudal dues], Volume 4, conclusion. These contradictions arise in Maurer: (1) from his habit of bringing in evidence and examples from all periods side by side, and jumbled together; (2) from the remnants of his legalistic bias, which always gets in his way whenever it is a question of understanding a *development*; (3) from his great lack of regard for the part played by *force*; (4) from his enlightened prejudice that since the dark Middle Ages a steady progress to better things *must* surely have taken place—this prevents him from seeing not only the antagonistic character of real progress, but also the individual retrogressions.

You will find that my thing is by no means all of a piece but a regular patchwork. The first draft was all of one piece but unfortunately wrong. I only mastered the material by degrees and that is why there is so much patching together.

Incidentally the general reintroduction of serfdom was one of the reasons why no industry could develop in Germany in the seventeenth and eighteenth centuries. In the first place there was the *reversed* division of labour among the gilds—the opposite from that in manufacture: the work was divided *among the gilds* instead of inside the workshop. In England at this stage migration to the territory outside the gild took place, but in Germany this was prevented by the transformation of the country people and the inhabitants of the agricultural market towns into serfs. But this also caused the ultimate collapse of the trade gild as soon as the competition of foreign manufacture arose. The other reasons which combined with this holding back German manufacture I will here omit.

ENGELS TO MARX,
DECEMBER 16, 1882

THE point about the almost total disappearance of serfdom—legally or actually—in the thirteenth and fourteenth centuries is the most important to me, because formerly you expressed a divergent opinion on this. In the East Elbe region the colonisation proves that the *German* peasants were free; in Schleswig-Holstein Maurer admits that at that time "all" the peasants had regained their freedom (perhaps rather later than the fourteenth century.) He also admits that in South Germany it was just at this period that the bondsmen were best treated. In Lower Saxony more or less the same (e.g. the new *Meier* [tenant farmers] who were in fact copyholders). He is only opposed to Kindlinger's view that serfdom first *arose* in the sixteenth century. But that it was newly reinforced after that, and appeared in a second edition, seems to me indubitable. Meitzen gives the dates at which serfs begin to be mentioned again in East Prussia, Brandenburg, Silesia the middle of the sixteenth century; Hanssen gives the same for Schleswig-Holstein. When Maurer calls this a *milder* form of serfdom he is right in comparison with the ninth and eleventh centuries, when the old Germanic slavery still continued, and right too with regard to the legal powers which the lord also had then and later—according to the law books of the thirteenth century—over the serfs. But compared with the *actual* position of the peasants in the thirteenth, the fourteenth and, in North Germany, the fifteenth centuries, the new serfdom was anything but an alleviation. Especially after the Thirty Years' War! It is also significant that while in the Middle Ages the degrees of servitude and serfdom are innumerable, so that the *Mirror of Saxony*[1] gives up any attempt to speak of *egen lüde recht* [rights over owned people— i.e. bondsmen] this becomes remarkably simple after the Thirty Years' War.

ENGELS TO MARX, DECEMBER 22, 1882

I am glad that on the history of serfdom we "proceed in agreement", as they say in business. It is certain that serfdom and bondage are not a peculiarly medieval-feudal form, we find them everywhere or nearly everywhere where conquerors have the land cultivated for them by the old inhabitants—e.g. very early in Thessaly. This fact has even misled me and many other people about servitude in the Middle Ages; one was much too much inclined to base it simply on conquest, this made everything so neat and easy. See Thierry among others.

The position of the Christians in Turkey during the height of the old Turkish semi-feudal system was something similar.

---

[1] *Der Sachsenspiegel*—the legal code of the period.

Index

Index

(Figures in italic type refer to texts by Marx or Engels, others to the Introduction.)